Developing Basic Writing Skills

Developing Basic Writing Skills in English as a Second Language

Marie Hutchison Eichler

UNIVERSITY OF PITTSBURGH PRESS
for the
ENGLISH LANGUAGE INSTITUTE
of the
UNIVERSITY OF PITTSBURGH

TO MICHAEL EICHLER

Pitt Series in English as a Second Language—11
Published by the University of Pittsburgh Press, Pittsburgh, Pa. 15260
Copyright © 1981, University of Pittsburgh Press
All rights reserved
Feffer and Simons, Inc., London
Manufactured in the United States of America

Library of Congress Cataloging in Publication Data

Eichler, Marie Hutchison.
   Developing basic writing skills in English as a second language.

   (Pitt series in English as a second language)
   1.   English language—Text-books for foreigners.
2.   English language—Composition and exercises.
I.   Title.   II.   Series.
PE1128.E35   428.2′4   81-3068
ISBN 0-8229-8211-0 (pbk.)   AACR2

CONTENTS

INTRODUCTION

This text accompanies MMC: Developing Communicative Competence in English as a Second Language, by Mary Newton Bruder. It is intended for students in a basic writing course. The teaching points follow the general order of presentation used in MMC although some changes have been made. Ideally, the text reinforces the student's grammar class and develops sentence level writing ability. However, the text is complete in itself.

Each lesson begins with a model composition which illustrates the current teaching points and utilizes the past ones as much as possible. The model is about the general topic of the lesson and also presents vocabulary which the student may need during the lesson.

The model is followed by a Grammar section which begins with a Discovery procedure. This elicits the basic elements of the Grammar explanation. By looking at sample sentences and answering the questions below, the students should be able to formulate a basic rule for the grammatical pattern.

A Generalization follows the Discovery. It restates the basic elements of the Grammar point and provides further information and examples as needed. It is divided into the form and use of the point.

A Practice section follows the Generalization. It gives the student basic practice in manipulating the teaching point within sentences. These exercises typically consist of fill-in-the-blanks or rewrite transformations of sentences or of the model, although other exercises appropriate to the teaching point also occur.

The Discovery-Generalization-Practice group occurs two or three times in each lesson, depending on the number of teaching points. The end of the last practice is followed by ***. At this point, the student should stop work and obtain a copy of the answer key in the teacher's manual to correct his/her work. Self-correction is an important component of a writing class, and it is important that the student do it before he/she continues on to the more difficult work. If students are not working independently or if the teacher prefers to correct all exercises, the teacher should correct them before the student continues. Notice also, some of these exercises cannot be included in the answer key due to their nature.

The More Practice section follows the Grammar section. It provides more meaningful use of the teaching points in language that the student has created, although there is still some control. This section introduces use of the Grammar points in paragraphs written by the student. It should be remembered that students are only expected to show ability in sentence level work. Paragraph work only exists to allow the student to use the Grammar points more communicatively. The last assignment of the lesson, a composition, gives the student a chance to be as communicative as possible within a lesson framework. It is recommended that the teacher also assign free compositions occasionally. See the teacher's manual for suggested topics.

The teacher's manual contains more details about the theory, classroom application, suggested uses, notes about individual lessons, and the answer key.

ACKNOWLEDGMENTS

Many people have given expert help in the writing and formulation of this text. At the top of the list is Mary Bruder, who spent many hours analyzing each word. Patricia Furey was instrumental in helping with the first crucial classroom uses and she offered many helpful comments. Christina Paulston and Sarah Thomason also provided many valuable comments. My heartfelt thanks go to each of these people as well as the teachers who used the materials and offered suggestions, especially Ellen Douglas.

MHE
June, 1981

Developing Basic Writing Skills

LESSON 1   Simple Present Be
            Adjectives and Nouns
            Subject-Verb-Completer Sentences

INTRODUCTION

The Seasons in the Northern United States

In the northern U.S., June, July, and August are warm months. The flowers are open and colorful. The weather is pleasant. It is summer. September, October, and November are the autumn months. The trees are green, gold, red, and brown. The temperature is cool. The winter months are December, January, February, and March. December is cold. January, February, and March are very cold. The wind is strong. The snow is heavy. The hills and mountains are bright with snow. The trees are bare. April and May are the spring months. The weather is warm in the spring. The trees are green. The flowers are open again. April is the rainy month. May is the month of flowers. People are in the sun. They are happy.

GRAMMAR 1: Simple Present Be

    Discovery: 1. Three trees are green.
                2. John is a student.
                3. You are a nature lover.
                4. I am a teacher.

    A. Look at sentence 1. What is the subject? _____
        Is it singular or plural (one or many)? _____
        What is the verb? _____
        Write a rule. We use are when the subject is _____.

    B. Look at sentence 2. What is the subject? _____
        Is it singular or plural? _____
        What is the verb? _____
        Write a rule. Use is when the subject is _____.

    C. Look at sentence 3. What is the subject? _____
        What is the verb? _____
        Write a rule. Use are when the subject is _____.

    D. Look at sentence 4. What is the subject? _____
        What is the verb? _____
        Write a rule. Use am when the subject is _____.

1

```
┌─────────────────────────────────────────────────────────────────────┐
│ GENERALIZATION                                                        │
│                                                                       │
│ Form:   The personal pronouns are:                                    │
│                                                                       │
│         singular      plural        NOTE:  You can be singular or plural. │
│            I            we                                            │
│           you          you                                           │
│           he ⎞                                                        │
│           she ⎬        they                                          │
│           it ⎠                                                        │
│                                                                       │
│ Use am for the subject I.          I am happy now.                    │
│                                                                       │
│ To form negative sentences with be,   It is not warm in December.     │
│ write not after the verb.             The flowers are not open.       │
│                                       I am not from Pennsylvania.      │
└─────────────────────────────────────────────────────────────────────┘
```

PRACTICE

Exercise 1: Look at the paragraph on page 1. Draw a line under the subject
of each sentence. Circle each verb.

Ex: In northern U.S., June, July, and August (are) warm months.

Exercise 2: Fill in the blank with is, are, or am.

Ex: The weather ___is___ perfect.

1. Autumn _____ a beautiful season.

2. The sun _____ very bright.

3. Spring and summer _____ the favorite seasons.

4. I _____ from Vermont.

5. Vacations _____ great.

6. The students _____ happy in the summer.

7. Today _____ a beautiful day.

8. Colorado and Wyoming _____ mountainous states.

9. The trees _____ bright green.

10. You _____ from a warm country.

11. July _____ a hot month in Arizona.

12. The temperature and humidity _____ high in the summer.

13. The hills _____ white with snow.

14. I _____ a nature lover.

15. Winter in New England _____ very severe.

16. John and I _____ tourists.

17. Spring flowers _____ very delicate.

18. Southern California _____ warm and dry.

19. You _____comfortable in the summer.

20. Autumn colors _____ pretty.

Exercise 3: Rewrite the sentences in Exercise 2. Change them to the negative.

Ex: The weather is perfect.

The weather is not perfect.

GRAMMAR 2: Adjectives and Nouns

Discovery

	Nouns		Adjectives
Singular (one)	Plural (many)		
boy	boys		blue
vacation	vacations		cold
church	churches		beautiful
kiss	kisses		difficult

1. high temperature
2. good students

A. Look at number 1. What is the noun? _____

What is the adjective? _____

Is the adjective before or after the noun? _____

B. Look at number 2. What is the noun? _____

What is the adjective? _____

Is the adjective before or after the noun? _____

C. Look at the noun list above. What is the plural form of boy? _____

of vacation? _____

What letter do we add to make the plural form? _____

What is the plural form of church? _____

What is the plural form of kiss? _____

What letters do we add to these words for the plural form? _____

D. Compare numbers 1 and 2 above. Is the adjective form the same for singular and plural nouns? _____

GENERALIZATION

Form: A noun is a word for a person, place, thing, or idea.

    doctor (person)
    New York (place)
    tree (thing)
    love (idea)

An adjective describes a person, place, thing, or idea. It comes before the noun or in the completer (see Grammar 3).

    a good doctor
    noisy New York
    a green tree
    wonderful love

Most plural nouns end with -s.

doctor	doctors
tree	trees

Nouns which end with s,z,sh,x, or ch (when pronounced [č]) have es plural.

kiss	kisses
buzz	buzzes
wish	wishes
box	boxes
inch	inches

Nouns which end with y change to ies in the plural.

baby	babies

A few nouns have irregular plural forms. Here are some important irregular nouns.

man	men
woman	women
child	children
person	people (usually)

PRACTICE

Exercise 4: Fill in the blanks with adjective + noun phrases to make sensible sentences. Use the list below.

Ex: The ___*quiet man*___ is very nice.

Adjectives		Nouns	
big	intelligent	class	person
dirty	quiet	bus	child
bad	clean	girl	flower
old	happy	teacher	student
new	blue	pen	man
red	small	party	book

1. The _____ is boring.   3. The _____ is exciting.

   _____   _____

   _____   _____

   _____   _____

2. The _____ is very interesting.   4. The _____ is too noisy.

   _____   _____

   _____   _____

   Exercise 5: Rewrite the sentences in Exercise 4. Change them to plural.

   Ex: The quiet man is very nice.

   The quiet men are very nice

GRAMMAR 3: Subject-Verb-Completer

   Discovery: 1. John is a student.
               2. John is happy.
               3. John is in Switzerland.
               4. John is a happy man.

   A. Look at all four sentences. Write the subject. _____, _____, _____,

                                                    and _____.

       Are the subjects first, second or last in the sentences? _____

   B. Write the verbs. _____, _____, _____, and _____.

       Where are they? _____

   C. The remaining parts are completers. What is the completer in sentence 1?

       _____

       Is student a noun or adjective? _____

   D. What is the completer in sentence 2? _____

       Is it a noun or an adjective? _____

   E. What is the completer in sentence 3? _____

   F. What is the completer in sentence 4? _____

```
GENERALIZATION

Form:  English sentences are usually subject-verb-completer.
                                     1      2       3

       The completer is a noun, adjective
       or a phrase.  It comes after the
       verb.

                                 1          2       3
                                 Subject    Verb    Completer
       Noun                      John       is      a student.
       Adjective + noun          He         is      a happy student.
       Adjective                 He         is      happy.
       Phrase                    John       is      in New York.
```

PRACTICE

Exercise 6: Arrange the words in each group. Make a sentence. Use the
correct form of be in the simple present tense. The subject
has a line under it.

Ex: cold
     Vermont   *Vermont is cold.*
     (be)

1. Tokyo
   an important
   (be)
   city

2. (be)
   a cultural center
   Pittsburgh

3. football
   American sport
   a favorite
   (be)

4. in Pittsburgh
   steel
   (be)
   important

5. (be)
   very changeable
   the weather

6. very cold
   (be)
   autumn
   not

7. the great lakes
   (be)
   very large

8. an economic fuel
   (be)
   natural gas

9. season
   a wonderful
   summer
   (be)

10. fun
    (be)
    big snowballs

11. (be)
    summer
    a warm
    season

12. a warm
    (be)
    Arizona
    state

Exercise 7: Fill in the blank with a completer. Use your own ideas.

Ex: English is *an interesting language.*

1. Mary is _____

2. The favorite seasons are _____

3. I am _____

4. The weather is _____

5. The sky and air are _____

6. Summer is _____

7. You are _____

8. The United States is _____

9. My country is _____

10. The flowers are _____

****

MORE PRACTICE

Exercise 8: Answer the following questions in your own words. Use complete sentences.

1. What are the warm months in the northern U.S? In your country?

2. Describe the weather in the autumn in the northern U.S. In your country?

3. Describe the trees in the northern U.S. In your country.

4. Describe the winter months in the northern U.S. In your country.

5. Describe the spring months in the northern U.S. In your country.

6. When are the people happy in the northern U.S.? In your country.

Exercise 9: Choose a word from the word list below. Fill in the blank. Use the correct form of <u>be</u>. Be sure to make a logical story.

Fernando _*is*_ a new _____ at the _____ . He _____ in the
     (be)   (noun)   (noun)   (be)

U.S. to study in the department of _____ . He _____ from _____ .
                      (noun)   (be)   (place)

Today _____ the first morning of _____ . Fernando _____
    (be)   (noun)   (be)

_____ . The buildings _____ very _____ . They _____
(adjective)   (be)   (adjective)   (be)

gray and _____ . Fernando is _____ . The room in his building
    (adjective)   (adjective)

_____ not easy to find. It _____ in a _____ building. Ten
(be)   (be)   (adjective)

_____ are in the room. They are _____ . The _____ _____
(noun)   (adjective)   (noun)   (be)

in the front of the room. Fernando is _____ . This is a _____
                    (adjective)   (adjective)

experience.

Word List

Adjectives		Nouns		
lost	small	student/s	the term	Peru
quiet	tall	university	week	
attentive	gray	medicine	day	
new	black	engineering	building	
nervous	late	business	teacher	
worried	difficult	class	Mexico	

Exercise 10: READ AND COMMENT. Read each sentence. Write 3 more sentences that comment on the first sentence. Use simple present <u>be</u>.

    Ex: John is not happy.

      A. *He is not healthy.*

      B. *The weather is cold.*

      C. *He is in a hard school.*

NOTICE: Sentences A, B, and C are about John and the reason for his unhappiness. These sentences give more information about the first sentence.

1. The weather is nice in my country.

    A.

    B.

    C.

2. John is very happy in warm weather.

    A.

    B.

    C.

3. Today is a beautiful day.

    A.

    B.

    C.

4. My favorite season is _____.

    A.

    B.

    C.

5. My family is very interesting.

    A.

    B.

    C.

Exercise 11: Australia's seasons are opposite from the seasons in northern U.S. Write a composition about the seasons in Australia. Talk about the same things as the introduction about the northern U.S.

Begin: *The warm months in Australia are December, ...*

COMPOSITION

Write a composition about the weather and seasons in your country. Use the model and exercises as examples.

LESSON 2   Present Continuous

INTRODUCTION

New Students

I am a new student in the United States. I am studying education at the
university. I am a teacher in Colombia. I am making friends in the United
States. They are studying at the University too. I am staying with an American
family. They are nice, friendly people. I am happy with the family. The house
is large and I am comfortable.

A friend is staying in the dormitory. He is not happy. The dormitory is
noisy and crowded. He is a serious student. He is in the library every night.
But the library is uncomfortable. A second friend is staying in an apartment. It
is nice, bright, and quiet. He is a kind, intelligent man. He is studying
engineering. He is planning to build houses and apartments.

GRAMMAR 1: Present Continuous

Discovery: 1. He is studying chemistry.

A. Look at number 1. The verb has two words. What are they? _____, _____
    Why do we write is? Because the subject is _____.
    What is the simple form of studying? _____
    What ending does studying have? _____

B. Write a rule. Present continuous has _____words. The first
    word is a form of the verb _____. The second word is a simple
    verb + _____.

```
┌─────────────────────────────────────────────────────────────────────────┐
│ GENERALIZATION                                                            │
│                                                                           │
│ Form:  Present continuous =            They are playing tennis.           │
│        be + simple verb + ing          He is visiting friends now.        │
│                                                                           │
│        A.  Verbs with e at the end      have            having           │
│            usually drop the e and       give            giving           │
│            add -ing.                     live            living           │
│                                                                           │
│        B.  Verbs with one vowel + one    sit             sitting          │
│            consonant at the end: double  plan            planning         │
│            the consonant and add -ing.                                    │
│                                                                           │
│            To form negative present      I am not studying Chinese.       │
│            continuous, write not after   We are not living in Toledo.     │
│            be.                                                            │
│                                                                           │
│ Use:   Use present continuous for actions  We are having a test now.      │
│        happening right now or in the       They are having a test tomorrow.│
│        near future.                                                       │
└─────────────────────────────────────────────────────────────────────────┘
```

PRACTICE

Exercise 1: Rewrite the first paragraph of the introduction. Change I to
Ernesto in the first sentence, and to he in all other sentences.

Begin: *Ernesto is a new student in the United...*

Exercise 2: Fill in the blank with the correct form of the present
continuous. Use the verb in parentheses.

Ex: I _____*am studying*_____ at school. (study)

1. Mary _____ at the cafeteria now. (eat)

2. John and Margaret _____ at the university. (study)

3. I _____ on McKee Street. (walk)

4. The girls _____ downtown. (go)

5. The man _____ in class. (sit)

6. The flowers _____ in the garden now. (grow)

7. Snow _____ on the mountain now. (fall)

8. Joe _____ in the engineering department this very minute. (work)

9. Jose _____ in the dormitory. (sleep)

10. Alejandra and Rene _____ at the restaurant. (eat)

11. You _____ silly. (act)

12.   The professors _____ in the office right now. (talk)

13.   The teacher _____ in the lounge. (work)

14.   He _____ at Sears now. (shop)

15.   Bob and Bill _____ downtown. (drive)

      Exercise 3: Fill in the blank with the negative form of the verb in parenthesis.

          Ex: I *am not studying* at school. (study)

1.   Mary _____ at the cafeteria now. (eat)

2.   John and Margaret _____ at the university. (study)

3.   I _____ on McKee Street. (walk)

4.   The girls _____ downtown. (go)

5.   The man _____ in class. (sit)

6.   The flowers _____ in the garden now. (grow)

7.   Snow _____ on the mountain now. (fall)

8.   Joe _____ in the engineering department this very minute. (work)

9.   Jose _____ in the dormitory. (sleep)

10.   Alejandra and Rene _____ at the restaurant. (eat)

11.   You _____ silly. (act)

12.   The professors _____ in the office right now. (talk)

13.   The teacher _____ in the lounge. (work)

14.   He _____ at Sears now. (shop)

15.   Bob and Bill _____ downtown. (drive)

      Exercise 4: Fill in the blank with the present continuous form of the verb in parentheses.

Today, the university students *are moving* into the dormitories. They
                                  (move)

_____ suitcases and they _____ furniture too. My friend
  (carry)   (bring)

_____ a new stereo tomorrow. He is my roommate. We _____
  (buy)   (look)

for curtains, sheets and towels tomorrow, too. Now we _____ very
                                                        (work)
hard. My friend _____ the floor and I _____ the
                    (clean)   (open)
suitcases. We _____ our room because we _____ a party
                (prepare)   (have)
this weekend.

****

MORE PRACTICE

    Exercise 5: Answer the following questions about yourself. Use complete
                 sentences and tell the truth!

        Ex: Are you studying English or Arabic now?

        I am studying English now.

1. Are you studying reading or writing now?

   _____

2. Are you living alone or with friends?

   _____

3. Are you living at the university or in an apartment?

   _____

4. Is your family in the U.S. or in your country?

   _____

5. Are you going home or to the cafeteria after class?

   _____

6. Is your friend studying Arabic or English?

   _____

7. Is your friend staying in a dorm or renting an apartment?

   _____

8. Is your teacher speaking Chinese or English?

   _____

9. Are you working or sleeping now?

   _____

10. Is your teacher teaching lab or writing now?

_____

Exercise 6: READ AND COMMENT. Read the first sentence and write three more sentences to give more information about the first sentence. Use simple be and present continuous verbs only.

Ex: I am studying Spanish.

A. I am going to Spain.
B. I am working very hard.
C. The grammar is not difficult.

1. John is not going downtown now.

   A.

   B.

   C.

2. Cathy is preparing for school.

   A.

   B.

   C.

3. I am studying hard.

   A.

   B.

   C.

4. We are making friends in the U.S.

   A.

   B.

   C.

5. I am going to a movie tonight.

   A.

   B.

   C.

Exercise 7: Write three paragraphs about your first day in class. Today is the
first day. Use the following outline.

1. Describe your trip to the campus. Are you walking or riding the bus?
Is the campus confusing? Are you lost?

2. Describe your class. Your teacher. The students. What are they
doing? Is the class easy or hard?

3. How are you feeling after class? Happy or upset? Are you
returning tomorrow?

Begin: *Today is the first day of class. I am
walking to the university....*

COMPOSITION

Write a composition about your new life in the United States.

LESSON 3   Going to Future

INTRODUCTION

A Weekend Trip

Next weekend, I am going to visit my friends. They are studying in New York City. We are going to eat in good restaurants, visit important sights, and see a play. The United Nations is going to be very interesting. I am going to see all the exhibits. We are going to go to the Statue of Liberty and climb to the top, too. We are not going to Central Park. My friends are staying in a very tall apartment building. We are going to see the park from the apartment.

I am going to visit Radio City Music Hall and Madison Square Garden too. The most important sight is Broadway. Drama is my hobby. I am going to see famous stars and drama critics. The trip is going to be very interesting.

GRAMMAR: Going to Future

Discovery: 1. They are studying in New York City.
            2. Next weekend, I am going to visit my friends.

A. Look at sentence 1. Is it present time or future time? _____
    What is the verb phrase? _____
    How do we form this type of verb? _____ + _____ +

    _____

B. Look at sentence 2. Is it present time or future time? _____
    What is the verb phrase? _____
    How do we form the future verb in sentence 2? _____ + _____ +
    _____ + _____

GENERALIZATION

Form: Future time = <u>be</u> + <u>going to</u> + verb   The weather is going to be
        A time word is not necessary, but   wonderful next weekend.
        one is often used.   We are going to see Central
                                                     Park tomorrow.

        Negative = <u>be</u> + <u>not</u> + <u>going to</u> +   I am not going to visit Boston.
        verb
                                                     She is not going to eat pizza
                                                     tomorrow.

Use: "Going to" + verb always shows future   He is visiting New York now.
        time.
                                                     She is going to visit New York
                                                     next month.

        Compare "going to" verb forms with   I am going home now.
        present continuous. Present   I am going home tonight.
        continuous can show future time   I am going to go home tomorrow.
        if a future time expression is
        used. (see Grammar 2)

PRACTICE

Exercise 1:   Rewrite the following sentences. Fill in the blank with the
              <u>going to</u> future form of the verb in parentheses. Add a time
              expression from the list below.

<u>TIME EXPRESSIONS</u>

next { week   in a few { days
       month   weeks
       year   months
       weekend   years

Ex: John ----- a student. (be)

John is going to be a student next year.

1. I ------ tickets to the new play. (get)

   _____

2. Joanne ------- very beautiful. (look)

   _____

3. John ------ his name. (change)

   _____

4. Martha and Rich ------ in Chicago. (work)

   _____

5. I ------ at the university. (study)

_____

6. We ---------English (learn)

_____

7. The snow ------ everywhere. (fall)

_____

8. Jack ------- in Pittsburgh. (practice)

_____

9. The girl ------ Chinese. (speak)

_____

10. We ------ a lecture about history. (attend)

_____

11. You ------ in Dallas. (live)

_____

12. They ------ at the Mall. (shop)

_____

Exercise 2: Rewrite the sentences in Exercise 1. Change them to the negative form.

Ex: John is going to be a student next year.

John is not going to be a student next year.

1. I ------ tickets to the new play. (get)

_____

2. Joanne ------ very beautiful. (look)

_____

3. John ------ his name. (change)

_____

4. Martha and Rich ---- in Chicago. (work)

_____

5. I ------ at the university. (study)

_____

6. We ------ English. (learn)

_____

7. The snow ------ everywhere. (fall)

_____

8. Jack ---- in Pittsburgh. (practice)

_____

9. The girl ------ Chinese. (speak)

_____

10. We ------ a lecture about history. (attend)

_____

11. You ------ in Dallas. (live)

_____

12. They ------ at the Mall. (shop.)

_____

Exercise 3: Fill in the blank with the correct form of the present continuous
or going to future. Use the verb in parenthesis.

Ex: We *are studying* English now. (study)

1. He _____ in Paris now. (eat)

2. She _____ a lecture in Russian. (give)

3. We _____ to the museums tonight. (go)

4. I _____ California now. (visit)

5. We _____ our friends to the new exhibit next week. (take)

6. We _____ a French movie now. (see)

7. Margaret and I _____ in Pittsburgh next year. (study)

8. Joe _____ his children to the museum now. (take)

9. The weather _____ wet and cold next week. (get)

10. My friends _____ to Florida now. (go)

11. You _____ the letter now. (send)

12. Joe and Sue _____ a baseball game next week. (watch)

13. We _____ the Liberty Bell in Philadelphia next summer. (visit)

14. The wind _____ a lot of noise now. (make)

****

MORE PRACTICE

Exercise 4: Rewrite the INTRODUCTION about a weekend trip. Your friend is going to visit you in your native city. Talk about the things you are going to see and do. Here is a list of possible things to see:

museums	buildings
parks	historical sites
sports	governments
stores	
streets, bridges	

Begin: *Next weekend, my friend is going to visit me. I am going to show him my city. We...*

Exercise 5: READ AND COMMENT. Read the sentences. Write two more sentences to give additional information. Use <u>going to</u> future when possible.

Ex: Inflation is rising in the U.S.

A. *Prices are going to be very high.*
B. *Food is going to be expensive.*

1. My brother is studying medicine.

   A.

   B.

2. My friend is visiting my native city.

   A.

   B.

3. I am preparing for a cold winter.

   A.

   B.

4. We are going to travel in the United States.

   A.

   B.

5. Rich and John are having a party tonight.

   A.

   B.

Exercise 6: Write a short composition about your new apartment, house, or room. Use the outline below.

   1. Where do you live? Is it nice or horrible? Describe it.
   2. Tell three good or bad points about it.
   3. Tell three things you are going to do to make your home nicer.

Exercise 7: Answer the letter from your friend below. Be sure to tell your friend about your new life in the U.S. Use simple be, present continuous, and going to future verbs only.

Dear Khalil, (or your name)

   I am at home, but next month, I am going to Ohio. I am going to study engineering there. My mother is crying right now because she is going to miss me very much. But I am very excited. How are your classes? Are you happy in the U.S.? When are we getting together? I am going to be in your city for a few days next week. Please write soon.

                                   Your friend,
                                   Jin

COMPOSITION

Write a composition about next weekend. What are you going to do?

LESSON 4   Be Questions
            Yes/No, Wh-

INTRODUCTION

Letters of Inquiry

Ramadan Asadi is an Egyptian student. He is studying education in Cairo.
He is interested in studying in the United States next year, but he needs information
about the university.

Dear Sir or Madam:

    I am studying in Cairo now. But I am going to study in your univer-
sity next year. Could you please answer some questions? What is the tuition?
Where are the foreign students living? Is the English program going to be
long? What are the programs at your university? I am interested in education
and sociology. Are these programs going to be available? Thank you for
your help and time.

                Sincerely yours,

                Ramadan Asadi

                Ramadan Asadi

GRAMMAR 1: Yes/No Questions

    Discovery: 1. Is he a student?

    A. Look at sentence 1. What is the subject? _____

        Is it first or second? _____

    B. What is the verb? _____

        Is it first or second? _____

    C. Write a rule. For questions with be, the first word is the _____.
        The second word is the _____.

        2. Are they studying education or sociology?

    A. What is the subject in sentence 2? _____

        Is it first or second? _____

    B. What is the first verb word? _____

        Is it the first, second or third word in the question? _____

C. What is the main verb? _____

    Is it the first, second or third word in the question? _____

D. Write a rule. For present continuous questions, a form of <u>be</u> is first,

    the second word is the _____, and the third is the _____.

       3. Are we going to visit friends?

A. Look at the example. What is the first verb word? _____

    Is it the first, second, or third word in the question? _____

B. What is the subject? _____

    Is it the first, second, or third word in the question? _____

C. What are the other verb words? _____

    Are they first, second or third in the question? _____

    Which verb word is the main verb? _____

D. Write a rule. For "going to" questions, the first word is a form of

    _____, the second word is the _____, and the third

    phrase is _____ + _____ + the main verb.

GENERALIZATION

Form: <u>be</u> + subject (+ verb words)
       + completer

                             Is she sick?
                             Are they coming now?
                             Is John going to study
                                tomorrow?

Use: Use this question form when you   Is she sick?   Yes. (No.)
     want a <u>yes</u> or <u>no</u> answer.

PRACTICE

    Exercise 1: Make questions from each of the following groups. Pay attention
               to the time expressions to choose the <u>correct verb tense.</u>

        Ex: the director/help/the students/next week

          Is the director going to help the students next week?

        the programs/be/good

          Are the programs good?

        the teacher/come/now

          Is the teacher coming now?

1. you/write/a letter now

_____

2. the English programs/be/expensive

   _____

3. John attend/this school/now

   _____

4. the university/be/modern

   _____

5. you/meet/the director/next month

   _____

6. she/talk/to an advisor/now

   _____

7. the students/live/in the dormitories/next term

   _____

8. the dormitories/be/too crowded

   _____

9. the tuition/rise/next term

   _____

10. Mark/study/chemistry/now

    _____

11. You/apply/next year

    _____

12. the application/be/complete

    _____

13. John/ride/the bus to school/now

    _____

14. Mary/study/in North Carolina/now

    _____

15. the classrooms/be/large

    _____

GRAMMAR 2: <u>Wh-</u> Questions/Completer

Discovery:

Group A	Group B
1. He is studying something	What is he studying?
2. They are talking to somebody.	Who are they talking to?
3. She is coming sometime.	When is she coming?
4. They are going to visit somewhere.	Where are they going to visit?

A. What are the completers in Group A? _____, _____, _____, _____

B. What words ask about the completers in Group B? _____, _____, _____, _____

C. Compare the verbs in Group A with the verbs in Group B. Do they change?
   _____, they agree with the _____.

D. Write a rule. Use _____, _____, _____, _____
   to ask about the completer in questions. The verbs agree with the
   _____.

GENERALIZATION

Form: <u>wh-</u> word + <u>be</u> + subject   When are they going?
     (+ other verb word) + completer   Where is she now?

     Notice <u>be</u> agrees with the subject.

Use: Use the completer question form to   Where are the foreign
      ask for new information about the   students living? (in the
      completer.   dormitories)

          where ---------- places
           when ---------- times
            who ---------- people
           what ---------- things

PRACTICE

Exercise 2: Here is the first word of a sentence. Write <u>Q</u> if it is a
             <u>question</u>. Write <u>S</u> if it is a <u>statement</u>. Then complete the
             sentence.

             Ex: _Q_   Who _is the new teacher_?

1. _____   What _____

2. _____ Is _____

3. _____ Mary _____

4. _____ I _____

5. _____ Are _____

6. _____ Who _____

7. _____ Am _____

8. _____ Where _____

9. _____ People _____

10. _____ We _____

Exercise 3: Make a <u>wh-</u> question for the following statements about the completer.

Ex: Bob is living somewhere.

Where is Bob living ?

1. Jane and Joe are going to talk to somebody.

   _____

2. Margaret is buying a house sometime.

   _____

3. The girls are going somewhere.

   _____

4. Jane is asking for something.

   _____

5. John and Jim are going to go to Canada sometime.

   _____

6. Sally is writing something.

   _____

7. He and Jane are going to stay with somebody.

   _____

8. Ms. James is visiting the Institute sometime.

   _____

9. They are walking with somebody.

    _____

10. Ian is going to start something.

    _____

11. The puppy is going to eat something.

    _____

12. They are eating sometime.

    _____

GRAMMAR 3:   Wh- Questions/Completer

    Discovery: 1.   Something is dirty.
                 2.   What is dirty?
                 3.   Somebody is going to the museum.
                 4.   Who is going to the museum?

A. Look at sentence 1. What is the subject? _____

    Look at sentence 2. What question word asks about the subject of 1? _____

B. Look at sentence 3. What is the subject? _____

    Look at sentence 4. What question word asks about the subject of 3? _____

C. Look at sentences 2 and 4. Are the verbs before or after the question

    words? _____

D. Which question word is for people? _____ for things? _____

E. What is the verb in the questions? _____ is it -s form or

    simple form? _____

F. Write a rule. Use _____ and _____ to ask about the

    subject. These words are _____ in the question. The verb is

    _____ form.

GENERALIZATION

Form: Wh- word + is (+ other verb words)   Who is going?
       + completer. Notice: we use the   What is expensive?
       -s form of the verb (is).

Use: Use this question form when a specific   What is the price? ($800)
       subject is not mentioned. This question
       form asks for new information about the
       subject. Use who to ask about people,
       what to ask about things and animals.

PRACTICE

Exercise 4: Change the following statements to questions about the subject.

Ex: Something is lost.

What is lost ?
_____

1. Somebody is going to be very happy.

_____

2. Somebody is working in Pittsburgh.

_____

3. Something is on the blackboard.

_____

4. Somebody is going to class now.

_____

5. Somebody is helping the teacher.

_____

6. Something is due early.

_____

7. Somebody is going home.

_____

8. Somebody is working in the dormitory.

_____

9. Somebody is bored.

_____

10. Something is going to be easy.

_____

11. Something is difficult.

_____

12. Something is a lot of fun.

_____

Exercise 5: Change the following statements to questions about the subject or completer.

Ex: He is going somewhere.

Where is he going?

1. Something is going to be confusing.

_____

2. Tuition payments are due sometime.

_____

3. Jim is working somewhere.

_____

4. Somebody is going to live in an apartment.

_____

5. John is driving to the store sometime.

_____

6. Somebody is going to the movies.

_____

7. Something is on my desk.

_____

8. Jane is looking for something.

_____

9. Somebody is going to travel to Spain.

_____

10. Something is in the mailbox.

_____

11. Somebody is going to stay with friends.

_____

12. Cindy is working somewhere.

_____

****

MORE PRACTICE

Exercise 6: READ AND COMMENT. Read each sentence. Write 3 possible questions (yes/no or wh-) to get additional information.

Ex: He is studying English.

A. *Where is he studying?*

B. *Who is the teacher?*

C. *Is he learning a lot?*

1. I am going to study in an American University.

A.

B.

C.

2. My family is going to visit the U.S.

A.

B.

C.

3. José is staying with a family.

A.

B.

C.

4. The English program is very difficult.

A.

B.

C.

5. My native country is beautiful.

A.

B.

C.

6. Hotels in Mexico City are very nice.

   A.

   B.

   C.

7. John is making travel arrangements.

   A.

   B.

   C.

8. The students are living in dormitories.

   A.

   B.

   C.

   Exercise 7: Write a letter to an American friend. Tell him/her about your new life. Ask him/her about his/her life, etc.

   For example, ask about: family
                               school
                               job
                               news about your friends

   Use the following form for your letter:

   Today's date

   (your friend's name)

   . . . .
   . . . .
   . . . . etc.
                               (your name)

COMPOSITION

Write a letter to a travel agency. Ask questions about traveling to your favorite vacation country.

LESSON 5   Simple Present
          Possessives
          Demonstratives

INTRODUCTION

American Presidential Campaigns

American citizens elect their presidents every four years. But the interesting
part of each election is the campaign. The campaign is a time of persuasion. It
is long and very lively. During this time the candidates promise everything.
They appear on television and make their promises. They also criticize the other
candidates. The voters listen and remember, but they do not believe everything.

The height of the campaign is the debates. These discussions of the issues
are on television sometimes. The candidates wear good clothes and also makeup.
They stand tall and try to appear "presidential" and calm. Reporters ask difficult
questions. The candidates consider the questions and rarely answer. Instead,
they repeat their speeches. The voters become angry, the reporters choose a
"winner," and the campaign continues.

The best fun of a campaign is the mistakes. Sometimes a candidate says careless
things. The reporters love this and report these things every day. These mistakes
probably do not change the vote much, but they make life horrible for the future
president who says them. They also make the campaigns very interesting.

GRAMMAR 1: Simple Present

   Discovery: 1. Sometimes, a candidate says careless things.
               2. The candidates promise everything.

   A. Look at sentence 1. What is the subject? _____
       What is the verb? _____
       Is this verb simple form or -s form? _____
   B. Look at sentence 2. What is the subject? _____
       What is the verb? _____
   C. Write a rule. Third person singular subjects take verbs ending in _____.
       Verbs for other subjects are in the _____ form.

32

GENERALIZATION

Form: I, you, we, they and plural noun   Reporters ask difficult questions.
        subjects take the simple verb form.   We vote every four years.

        He, she, it and singular noun   The candidate stands tall.
        subjects take the -s verb form.   My neighbor votes in every election.

        Negative = do + not + simple verb.

        I, you, we, they and plural noun   I do not like the candidates.
        subjects take do.

        He, she, it and singular noun   My wife does not vote.
        subjects take does.

        Verbs that end with s, sh, z or   miss   misses
        ch take an -es ending.   wash   washes
                                                  buzz   buzzes

        Verbs that end with y change y   study   studies
        to i and add -es. (These are   cry   cries
        the same rules as plural nouns.)

        NOTE: I have, she has

Use: The simple present tense shows   Americans vote every four years.
        habitual actions or states and   Reporters often ask difficult
        actions or states which occur   questions.
        many times.

        Compare simple present with   The candidate speaks every day.
        previous patterns. Notice   The candidate is speaking now.
        the time expressions.   The candidate is going to speak
                                                    next week.

PRACTICE

Exercise 1: Fill in the blank with the correct simple present form of the verb
             in parentheses.

        Ex: I _live_ in New Mexico. (live)

1. People _____ a good debate. (love)

2. Senators _____ work at one o'clock. (begin)

3. The workers _____ safe jobs. (want)

4. We _____ politics in school every day. (study)

5. He _____ my opinion. (know)

6. I _____ in every election. (vote)

7. The president _____ a Volkswagon. (drive)

8. A voter _____ the best candidate. (choose)

9. An American _____ the right to vote. (have)

10. Congressmen _____ in many elections. (run)

Exercise 2: Fill in the blank with the simple present, present continuous, or underline going to form of the verb in parentheses.

Ex: He __*eats*__ pizza every night. (eat)

1. He _____ to the movies on weekends. (go)

2. Mr. Jackson _____ his dinner now. (eat)

3. I _____ a house next year. (buy)

4. We _____ our taxes now. (do)

5. They _____ at the meeting this very minute. (speak)

6. The Johnsons _____ all the time. (vote)

7. Margaret _____ for the presidency now. (run)

Exercise 3: Fill in the blanks with the correct form of the verb in parentheses. Pay attention to the time expressions. Use simple present, present continuous, or going to future forms.

Ex: John __*drinks*__ coffee every morning. (drink)

The Presidential Breakfast

Every Wednesday, the president _____ breakfast with his advisors.
(have)

They _____ national problems. The advisors _____ the president
(discuss)   (give)
important advice.

Right now, they _____ eggs and toast. They _____
(eat)   (discuss)
economic problems. The economic advisor _____ about inflation. He
(speak)

always _____ about inflation. It _____ an important problem.
(talk)   (be)

But the energy advisor _____ impatient. He _____ a new law next
(be)   (suggest)

week. He _____ to talk about it now. But the economic advisor
          (plan)

_____ too much time. Next Wednesday, the energy advisor _____
   (use)   (begin)

first.

Exercise 4: Fill in the blanks with simple present or present continuous forms
             of the verb in parentheses.

Joseph Wisnowski __*lives*_____ in New York City. He _____
                     (live)   (be)

a senator. He _____ a small constituency. Every six years, Joseph
                  (have)

_____ for the senate. Now, he _____ in an election. His
        (run)   (run)

daughter _____ with publicity every day. This morning, he _____
            (help)   (appear)

on television. Television interviews always _____ good publicity. This
                                                (give)

afternoon, he _____ the people in his constituency. Joseph _____
                (visit)   (be)

an honest politician. He _____ the elections every time.
                             (win)

Exercise 5: Rewrite the sentences in Exercise 1. Change them to the negative
             form.

             Ex: I live in New Mexico.
                  I do not live in New Mexico.

GRAMMAR 2: Possessive Adjectives

Discovery: 1. The advisor is with his secretary.
            2. The advisor is with his secretaries.

A. Look at sentences 1 and 2. Are the completers the same? _____
    The completer in 1 is _____
    The completer in 2 is _____

B. The possessive adjective is <u>his</u>. Does this change from singular to plural?

    _____

    Is it before or after the noun?_____

C. Write a rule. The possessive adjective is _____ the noun. It
    does _____ change forms.

GENERALIZATION

Form:

Subject Pronoun	Possessive Adjective	
I	my	The president has a large office.
you	your	He is in his office now.
we	our	
they	their	
he	his	I work on every election.
she	her	My job is easy but important.
it	its	

Use: Each possessive adjective has only one form. Use it before the noun, or before another adjective.

his room	his rooms
her staff	her large staff

PRACTICE

Exercise 6: Fill in the blank with the correct possessive adjective (my, your, our, their, his, her, its).

Today is a national election. The voters are going to choose _their_ future president, senators and judges. Mrs. Johnson is going to leave _____ home at 8:00 in the morning. She is going to cast _____ vote and go to work. _____ son Michael is twenty years old. He is not going to cast _____ vote. He thinks it is useless. The government doesn't follow the people's wishes before or after an election. Mr. Johnson is going to vote after work. He values _____ vote. He knows that _____ leaders are not always honest or the best. But he knows that _____ vote is _____ only power in government. Many Americans disagree with Mr. Johnson. They believe that _____ votes do not mean anything. In many elections, only fifty percent of Americans cast _____ votes.

Exercise 7: Fill in the blank with the correct possessive adjective (my, your, our, their, his, her, its).

The First Family

Christopher Eagles is the new president. _His_ wife, Julia, is _____ new first lady. They have two daughters. _____ daughters, Julia, and

Christina are_____ new first family.

Every day, the president works in _____ office. He meets foreign leaders, _____ personal advisors, and reporters. The reporters ask questions and the president answers _____ questions.

The first lady also works. She meets _____ staff, plans parties and sometimes advises _____ husband, the president. She also supports _____ favorite charities, usually children and art.

GRAMMAR 3: Demonstratives

Discovery: 1. This book is about politics. These books are about history.
2. That book is about China. Those books are about Cuba.

A. Look at the first pair of sentences. Which word is for singular nouns? This or these? _____
Are they before or after the noun? _____

B. Look at the second pair. Which word is for singular nouns? That or those? _____
Which is for plural nouns? _____ Are they before or after the noun? _____

GENERALIZATION

Form: this
that } + (adjective) + noun   This topic is difficult.
these   That topic is easy.
those   Those lazy voters do not vote.

Use: singular/near the writer   This candidate is a winner.
singular/far from the writer   That candidate is a loser.

plural/near the writer   These voters are voting now.
plural/far from the writer   Those voters are at home.

This and that also refer to previous
ideas, usually from the sentence   Inflation is rising too fast.
before.   This is the central idea.

PRACTICE

Exercise 8:   Rewrite the sentences below. Use <u>this</u> or <u>that</u> in the subject
according to the near/far cue.

Ex: The table is sturdy. (far)

That table is sturdy.

1. The senator is honest. (far)

_____

2. The political system is confusing. (near)

_____

3. The new presidential aide is very lazy. (far)

_____

4. The politician is a thief. (far)

_____

5. The governor wears T-shirts. (near)

_____

6. The congressman hires interesting secretaries. (far)

_____

7. The politician is successful. (near)

_____

8. The information is going to be necessary. (near)

_____

9. The adviser is becoming a problem. (far)

_____

10. The government is corrupt. (near)

_____

Exercise 9:   Rewrite your sentences in exercise 12. Change the subject to
the plural form. Make all necessary changes.

Ex: That table is sturdy.

Those tables are sturdy.

MORE PRACTICE

Exercise 10:   READ AND COMMENT. Write three pieces of additional information for each sentence below. Use possessive adjectives/pronouns and demonstrative adjectives when possible.

Ex: The governor drives a Volkswagon.

A. *This governor is very strange.*
B. *Our state does not have money.*
C. *Our governor is crazy.*

1. The president reads five newspapers every day.

    A.

    B.

    C.

2. The Kulaidan people pay high taxes.

    A.

    B.

    C.

3. I vote in every election.

    A.

    B.

    C.

4. Their government leaders have chauffeurs.

    A.

    B.

    C.

5. The president is going to study political science.

    A.

    B.

    C.

Exercise 11: Write three paragraphs about a popular person in your country. Answer the following questions in your paragraphs. Add other important information.

1. Who is this person? Where does he/she live? How old is he/she? What does he/she look like? (tall? dark? short? smiling? etc.)

2. Why is this person popular? Describe his/her personality (character). What is his/her job? (movies? government? education? sports? etc.) What popular things does he/she do in your country?

3. Do you like this person too? Why or why not? Do you know this person personally? (Is he/she a friend? acquaintance? a relative?)

Begin: *One popular person in my country is ...*

COMPOSITION

Describe the election process in your country.

LESSON 6   Count/Non-Count Nouns
            A lot/A little/A few/Much/Many
            Frequency Adverbs

INTRODUCTION

Changing American Families

The typical American, middle-class family usually has two parents and two
or three children. They live in a house. The father works in a company and the
mother works at home. The children go to school and they play with their friends.

But a lot of middle-class families are not typical. These families have
only one parent in the home because a lot of married couples divorce. Also,
a lot of mothers spend time at work. Forty-six percent of all adult women work
at least part-time.

A few families do not have any children. These "families" have only two
people. The adults choose to work full-time and live without children.

The new American family is not a typical one now. A lot of people worry
about the children and marriage. They know family changes are going to affect
other things, too.

GRAMMAR 1:   Count and Non-Count Nouns

GENERALIZATION

Count-nouns name things which we can   He has two brothers.
count.   I want a dozen flowers.

Non-count nouns name things which   I need advice.
we usually do not count. For   He is doing his homework.
example, advice, help, homework.
They are never in the plural form.

Below is a list of some nouns which are usually non-count:

food	energy	advice	art	air
bread	electricity	education	discipline	help
candy	gas	freedom	happiness	homework
coffee	oil	information	knowledge	money
meat		love	peace	paper
milk		respect	success	
rice		truth	work	
tea				
water				

NOTE: Time is a count noun when it   Joe called six times.
       means occasions.

       Time is a non-count noun when   I need time to study.
       it means duration.

PRACTICE

Exercise 1: Write the plural form of the nouns below if they are count.
            Write an X if they are usually non-count.

Ex: food __X__   boy _boys_

1. homework _____   11. money _____
2. family _____   12. child _____
3. suggestion _____   13. parent _____
4. advice _____   14. help _____
5. idea _____   15. change _____
6. information _____   16. couple _____
7. happiness _____   17. oil _____
8. friend _____   18. home _____
9. mother _____   19. man _____
10. death _____   20. success _____

GRAMMAR 2: Much/Many/A lot of

Discovery: A. Do you have much time?   I do not have much time.
                                           I have a lot of time.
                                           I have a little time.

            B. Do you have many friends.   I do not have many friends.
                                            I have a lot of friends.
                                            I have a few friends.

A. Look at Group A. Do we use much in affirmative sentences, negative
    sentences or questions? _____ and _____

B. Look at Group B. Do we use many in affirmative sentences, negative
    sentences or questions? _____ and _____

C. Is much before count or non-count nouns? _____
    Is many before count or non-count nouns? _____

D. Look at a lot of in Groups A and B. Is it used before count or non-count
    nouns? _____ a little? _____
    a few? _____

GENERALIZATION

Use <u>much/many</u> in questions and negative statements

<u>much</u> + non-count nouns

Does he have much time?
He does not want much advice.

<u>many</u> + count nouns

She does not go to many movies.
Does she talk to many people?

A <u>lot of</u> means the same as <u>much</u> and <u>many</u>.
Use <u>a lot of</u> with <u>all sentence types</u> and <u>count</u> or <u>non-count</u> nouns.

She has a lot of friends
Does she eat a lot of cheese?

She does not give a lot of advice.

Use <u>a little</u> and <u>a few</u> in affirmative statements and questions.

<u>a little</u> + non-count nouns

Do you want a little sugar?
I am going to give the boy a little advice.

<u>a few</u> + count nouns

Does she need a few ideas?
They want a few free days.

PRACTICE

Exercise 2: Fill in the blanks with the correct form of the noun in parentheses.

Ex: My wife does not want many *children* . (child)

1. Elderly people have a lot of _____. (problem)

2. Children need a lot of _____. (love)

3. A lot of _____ worry about their children. (parent)

4. Some families do not have much _____ or _____. (food, money)

5. A lot of people do not give much _____ to elderly people. (respect)

6. Children need a lot of _____. (discipline)

7. A lot of _____ have problems these days. (marriage)

8. Do children receive much _____ at school? (education)

9. People do not trust many _____. (school)

10. A lot of _____ does not hurt children. (work)

Exercise 3:   Fill in the blanks with a lot of, much, or many. Use examples of each.

Ex: *A lot of*_____ mothers work during the day.

1. People say schools do not provide _____ discipline.

2. _____ families have only one child.

3. Family changes are going to affect _____ things.

4. Does the typical American family have _____ children?

5. Do children need _____ education?

6. _____ fathers are very busy with work, too.

7. Do children have _____ responsibilities?

8. _____ women work part-time.

9. Parents often do not have _____ time for their children.

10. Children need _____ advice.

Exercise 4:   Fill in the blanks with a little or a few.

Ex: That child needs *a little* advice.

1. Single parents have _____ problems.

2. A lot of parents give their children _____ responsibilities.

3. Elderly people need _____ help from the government.

4. Children need _____ discipline.

5. Parents should visit the schools _____ times.

6. Some children receive only _____ education.

7. _____ families are very small.

8. _____ single parents have wonderful families.

9. Children need _____ time to learn.

10. Elderly people receive only _____ respect from young people.

GRAMMAR 3: Frequency Adverbs

Discovery: 1. The typical American family is usually small.
            2. Jimmy always wears a key.

A. Look at sentence 1. What is the verb? _____

What is the frequency adverb? _____

Is it before or after the verb? _____

B. Look at sentence 2. What is the verb? _____

What is the frequency adverb? _____

Is it before or after the verb? _____

C. Write a rule. Frequency adverbs (always, often, etc.) come _____

be. They come _____ all other verbs.

```
┌────────────────────────────────────────────────────────────────────────┐
│                                                                          │
│  GENERALIZATION                                                          │
│                                                                          │
│  Form:  Frequency adverbs come after       They always eat spaghetti on  │
│           be and before other verbs.          Sundays.                   │
│                                             She is never late for class. │
│                                             I do not often get up early.  │
│                                                                          │
│  Use:  Use these adverbs to show the number of times.                    │
│         Here is a list of the frequency adverbs in this lesson:          │
│                                                                          │
│           always                  100%                                   │
│           usually                  __                                    │
│           often                                                          │
│           frequently               __                                    │
│                                                                          │
│           sometimes                50%                                   │
│           occasionally             __                                    │
│                                                                          │
│           rarely  )                 5%                                   │
│           seldom  }  Negative                                            │
│           never   )                 0%                                   │
│                                                                          │
└────────────────────────────────────────────────────────────────────────┘
```

PRACTICE

Exercise 5: Rewrite the following sentences to form a paragraph. Change
             some of the sentences using the frequency adverb in parentheses.

Jimmy Miller is a "latch-key" child.

At school he wears a key on a chain around his neck. (always)

This is because his parents are at work when he comes home. (usually)

Jimmy comes home at 3:00 (usually) and fixes a snack.

He watches television for a short time (often) or he plays ball. (sometimes)

At 5:00 he comes home and starts dinner. (usually)

His mother prepares the dinner on weekends. (always)

On week days, Jimmy puts the dinner in the oven.

He makes a salad. (frequently)

Later he sets the table.

He washes the dishes, too. (sometimes)

His parents come home at 6:00. (usually)

Jimmy does not have brothers or sisters.

He does a lot of work in the house and he is unhappy about that. (occasionally)

But he understands the reason.

Jimmy is smart for a nine-year-old.

Begin: *Jimmy Miller is a "latch-key" child. At school he always wears a key...*

Exercise 6: Rewrite the following sentences using the frequency adverb in parentheses.

Ex: Jimmy does not like school. (never)

Jimmy never likes school.

1. People do not understand the problems of elderly people. (rarely)

   _____

2. Children do not understand divorce. (seldom)

   _____

3. Schools do not replace parents. (never)

   _____

4. Young children do not enjoy empty houses. (rarely)

   _____

5. "Latch-key" children are not very unhappy. (never)

   _____

6. Elderly people do not receive a lot of respect. (seldom)

   _____

7. The divorce process does not make children or parents happy. (rarely)

   _____

8. People do not have simple solutions to these problems. (never)

   _____

Exercise 7: Rewrite the following sentences to form a paragraph. Change the
* sentences by adding the frequency adverb of your choice.
Be careful with the meaning!

* Elderly people do not receive much respect in the U.S.

* Americans admire beautiful, healthy people who work.

  Elderly people are sixty-five years old or more.

* They retire when they are sixty-five.

* Their health is not good.

* They are no longer "beautiful."

* Young people do not listen to elderly people.

* They do not give the elderly much respect.

* They do not give them their seats on the buses.

* They do not obey their wishes.

  A few elderly people go to nursing homes.

* But these homes cost a lot of money.

* Elderly people are not happy in them.

  A lot of young people love their parents and grandparents.

* But they are very busy.

* They are not able to take care of their elderly relatives.

Begin: *Elderly people do not always receive much respect in the U.S. . . .*

****

MORE PRACTICE

Exercise 8: Construct 5 sentences each using <u>much</u>, <u>many</u>, <u>a lot of</u>, <u>a little</u>, and
<u>a few</u>. Use the words given in parentheses. Use questions and
affirmative/negative statements, according to the punctuation.

A. <u>much</u>

  1. (coffee) *Does she drink much coffee* _____ ?

  2. (advice) _____

  3. (help) _____ ?

  4. (time) _____ .

  5. (sugar) _____ ?

  6. (information) _____ .

B. <u>many</u>

   1. (friend) _____ .

   2. (idea) _____ ?

   3. (party) _____ .

   4. (family) _____ ?

   5. (suggestion) _____ .

   6. (cigarette) _____ ?

C. <u>a lot of</u>

   1. (people) _____ .

   2. (time) _____ ?

   3. (milk) _____ .

   4. (child) _____ ?

   5. (help) _____ .

   6. (money) _____ ?

D. <u>a little</u>

   1. (wine) _____ .

   2. (sugar) _____ ?

   3. (meat) _____ .

   4. (candy) _____ ?

   5. (bread) _____ .

   6. (air) _____ ?

E. <u>a few</u>

   1. (store) _____ ?

   2. (person) _____ .

   3. (parent) _____ ?

   4. (home) _____ .

   5. (story) _____ ?

   6. (newspaper) _____ .

Exercise 9: READ AND COMMENT. Read each sentence. Write three more sentences to give additional information. Use <u>much</u>/<u>many</u>/<u>a lot of</u>, <u>a little</u>/<u>a few</u>, or frequency adverbs when possible.

Ex: In general, children are very happy in the U.S.

A. *A lot of children are usually healthy and happy.*

B. *A few children are poor and sick.*

C. *The sick children need a lot of help.*

1. Education is very important to a country.

   A.

   B.

   C.

2. Elderly people have a lot of valuable experience.

   A.

   B.

   C.

3. A lot of mothers have jobs today.

   A.

   B.

   C.

4. People have a lot of free time today.

   A.

   B.

   C.

5. Government programs help a lot of people.

   A.

   B.

   C.

Exercise 10: Elderly people in the U.S. (over 65 years old) do not receive much respect sometimes. A lot of Americans value work and elderly people stop working (retire) at age 65. Now this is changing. We realize that elderly people have a lot of experience and knowledge. Our government is developing programs to help our elderly people now.

Write a composition about elderly people in your country. Answer the following questions.

1. How long do people work in your country? When do elderly people stop working (retire)?

2. What do people do after retirement? Where does their money come from? Do they live comfortably?

3. How do people in your country feel about elderly people? (respect? love? obedience to their wishes?) Is this changing? now? How do your young people feel about elderly people?

Begin: *People in my country...*

COMPOSITION

Write a composition about one of the following:

A. Families in your country.

B. Children in your country.

LESSON 7   Prepositional Phrases after the Noun
          Some/Any
          Indefinite Subject Pronouns (<u>every</u>/<u>no</u>)

INTRODUCTION

My Dreams

Everybody occasionally has a bad dream. Some people rarely have problems
in their sleep. I am not so lucky. I always have bad dreams. This does not
happen one time every night. Oh no! I have many bad dreams every night.

Try this example. I'm running in a room with very small furniture. Everything is running. The room has a small couch, a table, a chair and a television.
These pieces of furniture are only one foot tall. But they run very fast. (In
my dreams, everything always runs fast except me). The furniture is chasing me
around the room. It bites my ankles and crawls up my legs. The couch pulls
the hair on my legs. The whole situation is disgusting.

Or imagine this dream. I am eating a hamburger. Suddenly, my teeth are
alive. They talk a lot, but they do not allow my mouth to talk or eat. My
teeth are holding my tongue. They are laughing and joking. My teeth are having
fun. I am in misery.

This is always the case. I spend many nights of fear and frustration, and
in the daytime, I am a man with red eyes and a dazed mind.

GRAMMAR 1: Prepositional Phrases after the Noun

    Discovery: 1. I see the man. The man is in the room.
                2. I see the man <u>in the room</u>.

    A. Look at sentence 2. Who is in the room? _____
        Is this phrase before or after the noun it describes? _____

GENERALIZATION

Form: Many prepositional phrases come after the noun they
        describe. They often begin with prepositions like
        in, on, with, of, from, and about.

noun   + preposition + (a/the, my, this . .) + adjective + noun

the man   in   the   red   car
the person   with   green   eyes
a story   about   politics

Use: Use these prepositional phrases to   I know the man. The man is
        combine two thoughts in one   in the car.
        sentence.   I know the man in the car.

                                                  We see the children. The
                                                     children have the ball.
                                                  We see the children with
                                                     the ball.

                                                  She is eating ice cream.
                                                     The ice cream has choco-
                                                     late bits.
                                                  She is eating ice cream with
                                                     chocolate bits.

PRACTICE

Exercise 1:   Draw a line under each prepositional phrase. Circle
              the noun it describes.

Ex.   The couch pulls the (hair) on my legs.

1. Some people rarely have problems in their sleep.

2. Restful sleep in a good bed is very good medicine.

3. Dreams about beautiful people are very pleasant.

4. I spend many nights of fear.

5. The people in my dreams are always terrible.

6. My friend has dreams about beautiful trees and flowers.

7. I do not like nightmares with monsters.

8. Bob often has daydreams in biology class.

9. A lot of people have dreams about water.

10. I have a toy dog on my bed.

Exercise 2: Make **one** sentence from two. Use prepositional phrases.

Ex: I have that dream every night. It is about my childhood.

I have that dream about my childhood every night.

1. The girl has a problem. She has green hair.

   _____

2. I see monsters every night. The monsters are in my bed.

   _____

3. Jane has a lot of nice dreams. They are about handsome men.

   _____

4. A lot of people have interesting dreams. They are about running.

   _____

5. I often have bad dreams. They are in Latin.

   _____

6. I am running in a room. The room has small furniture.

   _____

7. My friend is in the hospital. She has blue teeth.

   _____

8. I always have silly dreams. They are about little men.

   _____

9. The yellow monster is chasing me. It has red eyes.

   _____

10. Dr. Psycho is writing a book. The book is about dreams.

    _____

Exercise 3: Rewrite the sentences in Exercise 1. Change them to the negative form.

Ex: The couch pulls the hair on my legs.

The couch does not pull the hair on my legs.

1. The girl has a problem. She has green hair.

   _____

2. I see monsters every night. The monsters are in my bed.

   _____

3. Jane has a lot of nice dreams. They are about handsome men.

   _____

4. A lot of people have interesting dreams. They are about running.

   _____

5. I often have bad dreams. They are in Latin.

   _____

6. I am running in a room. The room has small furniture.

   _____

7. My friend is in the hospital. She has blue teeth.

   _____

8. I always have silly dreams. They are about little men.

   _____

9. The yellow monster is chasing me. It has red eyes.

   _____

10. Dr. Psycho is writing a book. The book is about dreams.

    _____

GRAMMAR 2: Some/Any

    Discovery: 1. The family has some problems.
                2. Does the family have some problems?
                3. Does the family have any problems?
                4. They do not have any problems.

  A. Look at sentence 1. Where is some? Before the _____ .
      Is the noun (problems) singular or plural? _____
      Is the sentence affirmative or negative? _____

B.   Look at 2 and 3. Where are <u>some</u> and <u>any</u>? Before the _____.
     What kind of sentences are 2 and 3?   _____

C.   Look at 4. Is this sentence affirmative or negative? _____
     Do we use <u>some</u> or <u>any</u>? _____

D.   Write a rule. Use <u>some</u> in _____ sentences and _____.
     Use <u>any</u> in _____ sentences and _____.

GENERALIZATION

Form: Use <u>some</u> in affirmative statements.   I have some friends.
                                                           She wants some coffee.

       Use <u>any</u> in negative statements.   I do not have any time.
                                                           They do not need any ex-
                                                           planations.

       Use <u>some</u> or <u>any</u> in questions.   Do you have any time?
                                                           Does he see some people?

Use: Count or non-count nouns may   She needs some time. (non-
       follow <u>some</u> and <u>any</u>. Count nouns   count)
       take plural endings.   She needs some ideas. (count)
                                                           She does not want any advice.
                                                              (non-count)
                                                           She does not want any sug-
                                                              gestions. (count)

Exercise 4:   Fill in the blank with <u>some</u> or <u>any</u>.

        Ex: I often have *some*____ wonderful dreams.

1. Joe wants _____ milk.

2. Do you have _____ family problems?

3. We are going to see _____ houses in the valley.

4. I do not have _____ shirts.

5. Single parents do not have _____ free time.

6. Our company has _____ problems.

7. She knows _____ people in Chicago.

8. Margaret is not buying _____ tomatoes.

9. Do they need _____ money?

10. Joe and Bill want _____ help.

Exercise 5: Fill in the blank with the correct form of the noun in parenthesis.

Ex: We watch some *movies* _____. (movie)

1. Jane does not have any _____ in her dreams. (child)

2. We have some _____ in our dreams. (strange situation)

3. Some _____ are very long. (dream)

4. Are the children having any _____? (restless night)

5. He does not want any _____. (advice)

6. I never have any _____. (nightmare)

7. Is the doctor giving some _____? (suggestion)

8. The author writes some _____ every afternoon. (horror story)

9. Do they need any _____? (help)

10. You have some _____ for me. (idea)

GRAMMAR 3: Indefinite Subject Pronouns (Every/No)

Discovery: 1. All the people know John.
            2. Everybody knows John.
            3. No person knows John.
            4. Nobody knows John.

A. Look at sentence 1. What is the subject? _____

   Look at sentence 2. What is the subject? _____

   What does underlined everybody mean in sentence 2? _____

B. Look at sentence 3. What is the subject? _____

   Look at sentence 4. What is the subject? _____

   What does underlined nobody mean in sentence 4? _____

C. Does underlined every- or underlined no- mean "all"? _____

   Does underlined every- or underlined no- mean "no"? _____

D. Look at the verbs in sentences 2 and 4. Are they underlined -s form or simple

   form? _____

E. Write a rule. Use _____ in the subject to mean "all."

   Use _____ in the subject to mean "no."

   The verb is the _____ form.

GENERALIZATION

Form:

every + { body (all the people)
         { thing (all the things)

no + { body (no person)
      { thing (no thing)

These take the -s verb form.

(Note: everywhere, for places,
    is never the subject.)

Everything happens too fast.
Everybody is happy.
Nothing entertains unhappy
    people.
Nobody eats wood.

PRACTICE

Exercise 6: Answer the following questions. Use everybody/everything or
nobody/nothing, according to the beginning of the answer. Use
the same verb in your answer as the verb in the question.

Ex: Do you like homework? Of course not!

Nobody likes homework.

Do you like ice cream? Of course!

Everybody likes ice cream.

1. Do many people have nightmares?

    Of course! _____.

2. Do your friends hate parties?

    Of course not! _____.

3. Does the furniture run in your dreams?

    Of course! _____.

4. Is English class fun early in the morning?

    Of course not! _____.

5. Do your friends enjoy concerts?

    Of course! _____.

6. Do your teeth hold your tongue?

    Of course not! _____.

7. Do you always have bad dreams?

    Of course not! _____.

Exercise 6: (continued)

8. Do you always work?

Of course not! _____.

9. Is your friend excited about his thirtieth birthday?

Of course not! _____.

10. Do old songs sadden John?

Of course! _____.

Exercise 7: Fill in the blanks with correct form of the verb in parentheses.
Use simple present tense.

I often have the same dream again and again. In this dream, everybody _is_ ____
(be)
quiet and nobody _____. The people _____ in a circle in the
(move)   (stand)
middle of a forest. It _____ daytime. At noon, when the sun comes to the
(be)
middle of the sky, everybody _____ to sing my favorite song. I am
(begins)
standing near the people, but nobody _____ me. Everybody _____ for
(see)   (sing)
a long time and everybody _____happy. Soon one man _____ to the
(look)   (walk)
middle of the circle. Everybody _____ quiet. I _____ this
(become)   (watch)
performance, but I _____ not afraid. I _____ the people, but
(be)   (not recognize)
I _____them. Everybody _____ familiar. In the next
(know)   (seem)
minute, everything _____. Everybody _____ in a building now.
(change)   (be)
They _____ and _____. Everybody _____ a lot
(laugh)   (eat)   (make)
of noise. I always wake up at this point and I never understand this dream.

****

MORE PRACTICE

Exercise 8: READ AND COMMENT. Write 3 more sentences giving additional
information. Use phrases, some/any, and every/no pronouns.

Ex: Nightmares are frightening.

A. _Nightmares with monsters are bad._
B. _Some nightmares seem very real._
C. _Everybody hates nightmares._

1. Dreams have important meanings.

    A.

    B.

    C.

2. Horror movies are popular.

    A.

    B.

    C.

3. I sleep very badly.

    A.

    B.

    C.

4. I have wonderful dreams.

    A.

    B.

    C.

5. I am always tired in class.

    A.

    B.

    C.

Exercise 9: Write 3 paragraphs about the following dream. Use the facts below.
            You are the dreamer!

1. A yellow monster is chasing you. Describe the monster.
    Describe your feelings.

2. You meet a beautiful frog. He offers help. You hate frogs,
    (they are wet) but you need help. The frog wants a kiss first.
    (Yuck!)

3. The frog becomes a handsome man or woman. A prince/ss?
   A fairy? An angel? You are in love. What are your plans?
   Suddenly, you wake up. How do you feel?

   Begin: *I am running in a forest because a terrible monster is chasing me. It is...*

COMPOSITION

Write a composition about a common dream you frequently have (or make one up).

LESSON 8   Past <u>Be</u>
Simple Past

INTRODUCTION

My Life

I was born in 1950. I was the first child in my family. We lived in an
apartment in those days. It had three rooms, but my parents were lucky. I was
not a noisy child.

I began school six years later, and I hated it. My teachers were good, the
school was beautiful, but I was unhappy. My parents did not understand this.
Quiet children love school, they thought. I was an exception.

Soon, I liked my classes. Mrs. Simpson was my second-grade* science teacher.
She always smiled and she always had a kind word for me. She understood me. She
gave me extra attention. I often helped her in the lab.

Today, I am a microbiologist. My work and studies never finish, but I am happy.
Mrs. Simpson did not cause my career choice but she helped a lot. She probably
does not remember the shy child in her class years ago. I remember her very well.

_____

*   second year of elementary school

GRAMMAR 1: Past <u>Be</u>

Discovery: 1. I was the first child in my family.
2. My parents were lucky.
3. You were a noisy child.

A. Look at sentence 1. What is the subject? _____

Is it singular or plural? _____

What is the verb? _____

B. Look at sentence 2. What is the subject? _____

Is it singular or plural? _____

What is the verb? _____

C. Look at sentence 3. What is the subject? _____

What is the verb? _____

D. Write a rule. Use <u>was</u> with _____ subjects. Use <u>were</u> with

_____ subjects and _____.

61

```
GENERALIZATION

Form:

you  ⎫           I  ⎫              You were a student in 1963.
we   ⎬  were     he ⎬  was         They were healthy last week.
they ⎭           she⎮              I was unhappy.
                 it ⎭


Negative = was/were   not          He was not a good student.
                                   They were not happy children.


Use:  Was/were usually show past time.   I was unhappy in school
                                            last year.
```

PRACTICE

Exercise 1: Fill in the blank with the correct past tense form of be.

My father's family _____ in northern Ireland in the nineteenth century.
Three sons and four daughters _____ in a small house on a small piece of land.
The oldest son _____ Conor. He _____ tall and heavy. When his father died,
the land _____ his and Conor _____ an important man. Land _____
important in Ireland. The land _____ small and poor, but it _____
important.

The second son _____ Archie. Archie _____ not rich with land. When
he _____ eighteen years old, he went to Canada, and later to the United States.
In Ireland, a job _____ hard to find. In Canada, a man _____ able to make
a living.

The third son _____ Dary. Dary _____ quiet and very religious. He
_____ a small man. When he _____ fifteen years old, he entered the priest-
hood.

In Ireland, in the nineteenth century, a lot of families separated. The
country and people _____ poor. The best possibilities _____ in other countries.

Exercise 2: Fill in the blank with present or past tense be. Watch the
            time words.

                Ex: I ___*was*___ a student two years ago.

1. Joanne _____ my sister.

2. We _____ in Boston last Friday.

3. Joe and I _____ students now.

4. My family _____ in Ireland in the nineteenth century.

5. Mom and Dad _____ tyrants now.

6. I _____ in London last winter.

7. My uncles _____ in Pittsburgh for the World Series in 1979.

8. She _____ a student this semester.

9. Our new teacher _____ Venezuelan.

10. Her daughter _____ sick last week.

Exercise 3: Fill in the blank with the negative form of past be.

Ex: I *was not* a student two years ago.

1. Joanne _____ my sister.

2. We _____ in Boston last Friday.

3. Joe and _____ students now.

4. My family _____ in Ireland in the nineteenth century.

5. Mom and Dad _____ tyrants now.

6. I _____ in London last winter.

7. My uncles _____ in Pittsburgh for the World Series in 1979.

8. She _____ a student this semester.

9. Our new teacher _____ Venezuelan.

10. Her daughter _____ sick last week.

Exercise 4: Use the phrases below to make sentences. Use past be. Add more information telling when. Make time expressions from the list below.

TIME WORDS

last + { week / year / month (March, April, . .) / day (Saturday) / night

a year (2 years, 10 years, . .) }
a month (2 months, 6 months, .) } + ago
a week (2 weeks, 6 weeks, . .) }

Ex: I/ student

I was a student last year.

1. family/Spain _____

2. I/tired _____

3. houses/expensive _____

4. brother/sick _____

5. father and mother/Greece _____

6. the flowers/beautiful _____

7. Paris/exciting _____

8. the bus drivers/on strike _____

9. we/confused _____

10. birthday/noisy _____

GRAMMAR 2: Simple Past

Discovery: 1. Mrs. Simpson helped me.

A. What is the verb? _____

What is its simple form? _____

What is the past tense ending? _____

B. Write a rule. For simple past tense, add _____ to the form of the verb.

┌───┐

GENERALIZATION

Form: Simple past = verb + ed   I finished my studies in 1978.
(add only d if the simple
verb ends with e: live---   I liked my classes a lot.
lived)

Negative = did not + simple   Mrs. Simpson did not cause my
verb form.   career choice.

Use: Use simple past for actions   She always smiled.
which were completed (began   They helped me every day.
and ended), one time or many
times, in the past.

└───┘

Many important verbs are irregular in the past tense. Here is a partial list:

Present	Past	Present	Past
be	was/were	leave	left
become	became	lose	lost
begin	began	make	made
buy	bought	meet	met
come	came	read	read
drink	drank	say	said
do	did	see	saw
eat	ate	sit	sat
feel	felt	send	sent
find	found	speak	spoke
fly	flew	take	took
get	got	tell	told
give	gave	think	thought
go	went	understand	understood
have	had	write	wrote
hear	heard		

PRACTICE

Exercise 5: Fill in the blanks with the past tense form of the verb in parentheses.

When Michael _was_ nine years old, he _____ to a summer camp.
      (be)   (go)

His two friends, Bob and Don, _____ also. These three boys _____
                   (go)   (be)

best friends. They _____ everything together. During the day, they
              (do)

_____ baseball, _____ in the woods, and _____ stones. At
(play)   (walk)   (collect)

night, they _____ hotdogs, _____ stories, and _____ letters.
        (eat)   (tell)   (write)

Michael and his friends _____ to the camp every summer. But every year,
                     (go)

the camp _____. At first, it _____ wonderful and exciting. Michael
      (change)   (be)

_____ everything. But the years _____, Michael and his friends
(enjoy)   (pass)

_____ older, and the camp _____ a lot of fun. The camp
(get)   (be not)

_____ young, but the boys _____ adults.
(remain)   (become)

Exercise 6: Rewrite the following sentences. Change them to simple past tense. Change the time expression if necessary.

Ex: We go to New York every year.

We went to New York last year.

1. We travel to Guadelajara every February.

_____

2. My sister lives in St. Louis now.

_____

3. Our teacher takes us to the museum on Wednesdays.

_____

4. We are seeing Cairo next month.

_____

5. We attend the concert every week.

_____

6. Carlos writes to his girlfriend every week.

_____

7. We watch the movies at two o'clock.

_____

8. I sit with Carmen in class.

_____

9. They answer our questions every time.

_____

10. We are reading a book about Egypt now.

_____

Exercise 7: Rewrite your sentences in exercise 6. Change them to negative.

Ex: We go to New York every year.

We did not go to New York last year.

1. We travel to Guadelajara every February.

   _____

2. My sister lives in St. Louis now.

   _____

3. Our teacher takes us to the museum on Wednesdays.

   _____

4. We are seeing Cairo next month.

   _____

5. We attend the concert every week.

   _____

6. Carlos writes to his girlfriend every week.

   _____

7. We watch the movies at two o'clock.

   _____

8. I sit with Carmen in class.

   _____

9. They answer our questions every time.

   _____

10. We are reading a book about Egypt now.

   _____

****

MORE PRACTICE

Exercise 8: READ AND COMMENT. Read each sentence. Write 3 more sentences to give additional information. Use <u>past tense</u> verbs in your sentences.

Ex: I was born in New York City.

A. *My family was not rich.*
B. *We lived in a small apartment.*
C. *I saw a lot of movie stars there.*

1. Julio traveled a lot during college.

    A.

    B.

    C.

2. Jane visited her family last week.

    A.

    B.

    C.

3. Ms. Fisher became a doctor.

    A.

    B.

    C.

4. Mr. and Mrs. Petroboni wanted a new house.

    A.

    B.

    C.

5. The two sisters went on a vacation.

    A.

    B.

    C.

Exercise 9: Write a short composition about Marta Johannsen. Describe her early life. Add more information if necessary. Read all the information carefully first. Choose the information that you want for your composition.

NAME: Marta Johannsen

BORN: September 26, 1943. New York, New York

EDUCATION: Public School Number 53, 1948-1954
Martin Luther King High School, 1954-1960
University of Syracuse, 1960-1964

EMPLOYMENT: Waitress, Porkey's Restaurant, 1959-1960

Clerk, General Hospital, 1960-1962

Secretary, Brigham's Accounting, 1962-1964

Computer Programmar, IBM Corporation, 1964-present

FAMILY: Husband - Eric

Born: 1946, Buffalo, New York

Employment: Accountant, Brigham's Accounting,
1964 - present

Children: Linda and Peter (twins)

Born: 1966, New York, New York

Education: Public School Number 12, 1972-1978

Rafferty Junior High School, 1978-present

Begin: *Marta Johannsen was born on September 26, 1943 in New York City....*

COMPOSITION

Write a composition about your life.

LESSON 9   Answers to When
             Indefinite Pronoun Completers
             (Every-/Any-)
             Verb Review

INTRODUCTION

My Favorite Trip

During our vacation last year, my friend and I took a trip to New Orleans.
We went there on April 20 and returned on May 2. We chose these two weeks because
New Orleans is beautiful and warm in April.

We had such a good time! Our first night in the city, we went to Bourbon
Street and watched everything and everybody. We saw a very old man in the middle
of the street. He danced and his friend played some music. Later, they collected
money in their hats. We also heard some fine music. Al Hirt played his trumpet
in one club.

During our vacation, we also visited Jackson Square, near the Mississippi
River. It is large, beautiful, and often crowded. Artists sat on the sidewalks.
They sold their paintings and they drew pictures of the people. On the river,
a large steamboat, The President, sailed quietly. It was a beautiful picture.

Next year, in April, we're going to return. We're going to see everything
again, during the festival of Mardi Gras.

GRAMMAR 1: Answers to When

    Discovery: 1. I am leaving on Saturday.
                2. He was born on June 5, 1950.
                3. She is visiting the city on May 2.
                4. He was born in 1950.
                5. The celebration is going to begin in June.
                6. The U.S. was at war four times during the twentieth century.
                7. He was in Algeria during the war.
                8. My father was born during the earthquake.

    A. On, in, and during help answer questions with when.

        Which preposition is for days and dates that name the day? _____

        Which preposition is for months, years, and centuries? _____

        Which preposition is for events? _____

70

GENERALIZATION

Use: On, in and during begin phrases
that answer the question when.

Use on for specific days and dates, such as:	on Monday; on January 9; on July 4, 1779
Use in for dates with no specific day mentioned such as months, years, centuries, and seasons.	in June; in May, 1981; in the nineteenth century; in the spring; in 1904
Use during for general periods of time and events.	during the war; during the Depression; during the fire; during the ceremony
In and during may be used with the same expressions. We also use during to emphasize the length of time.	I was in Philadelphia $\left\{ \begin{array}{l} in \\ during \end{array} \right\}$ June There were many wars during the seventeenth century.

PRACTICE

Exercise 1: Fill in the blank with in, on, or during.

Ex: I was born *during* the Depression.

1. We are going to the park _____ Saturday.

2. I was born _____ January 15, 1948.

3. He was a scholar _____ the seventeenth century.

4. Many flowers bloom _____ the spring.

5. He was a soldier _____ the war.

6. _____ Monday, we are going to Kentucky.

7. They are going to leave _____ July.

8. Some people become depressed _____ the winter.

9. We were in New Orleans _____ Mardi Gras week.

10. Everybody celebrates _____ July 4th.

GRAMMAR 2: Indefinite Pronoun Completers (Every-/Any-)

Discovery: 1. We are studying all subjects.
            2. We are studying everything.
            3. He is not studying any subjects.
            4. He is not studying anything.

A. Look at sentence 1. What is the completer? _____

Look at sentence 2. What is the completer? _____

Are sentences 1 and 2 affirmative or negative? _____

What does <u>everything</u> mean in sentence 2? _____

B. Look at sentence 3. What is the completer? _____

Look at sentence 4. What is the completer? _____

Are sentences 3 and 4 affirmative or negative? _____

What does <u>anything</u> mean in sentence 4? _____

C. Do we use <u>every-</u> or <u>any-</u> in affirmative sentences? _____

Do we use <u>every-</u> or <u>any-</u> in negative sentences? _____

D. Write a rule. Use _____ in the completer when the sentence is <u>affirmative</u>. Use _____ in the completer when the sentence is <u>negative</u>.

GENERALIZATION

Form:

every-+ { <u>body</u> (all the people)   He sees everybody.
          <u>where</u> (all the places)   They go everywhere.
          <u>thing</u> (all the things)   I buy everything.

any-+   { <u>body</u> (no person)   She does not see anybody.
          <u>where</u> (no places)   We do not go anywhere.
          <u>thing</u> (no things)   You do not buy anything.

Use: Use <u>every-</u> in the completer in affirmative sentences.

Clara knows everybody.
John bought everything.

Use <u>any-</u> in the completer in negative sentences.

They rarely speak to anybody.
She does not go anywhere on vacation.

PRACTICE

Exercise 2: Answer the following questions. Use <u>everybody/-thing/-where</u> or <u>anybody/-thing/-where</u> in the completer. Use the same verb in your answer as the verb in the question.

Ex: Do you like ice cream?

Of course! *I like everything.*

Did you see the desert in California?

Of course not! *I did not see anything in California.*

1. Do you like to travel to foreign cities?

   Of course! _____

2. Did you tell your friend about the vacation plans?

   Of course not! _____

3. Are you going to see your friends when you arrive?

   Of course! _____

4. Is your friend going to fly to San Francisco?

   Of course not! _____

5. Do long airplane trips tire you?

   Of course! _____

6. Did you go to Cairo last week?

   Of course not!_____

7. Do you buy things during your vacations?

   Of course! _____

8. Do you want to see other cities in the U.S.?

   Of course! _____

9. Did you know everybody when you arrived in this city?

   Of course not! _____

10. Do you enjoy making plans about your vacations?

    Of course! _____

Exercise 3: Fill in the blanks with an every/any/no pronoun. Watch the meaning

Paul is planning an anniversary party for his wife. They were married five years ago. He told *everybody* about the party and _____ will come to his house to celebrate. Paul did not take his wife _____ last year. But this year he is planning a vacation as a gift. _____ knows this secret but _____ is going to tell his wife. It is a surprise.

By seven-thirty, _____ arrives at Paul's house. His wife, Ann, is not home. Paul cleaned _____ in the house. Almost _____ brought a present. The presents are on the table. Paul is very nervous about _____. At eight-fifteen, Ann comes home. _____ is quiet because they do not want Ann to hear them. Some people hide. They are excited about _____ too. Paul turns off the lights. When Ann comes into the house, Paul turns on the lights and _____ says "Surprise!" Ann did not suspect _____. She is very surprised.

GRAMMAR 3: Verb Review

```
┌─────────────────────────────────────────────────────────────────────────┐
│ GENERALIZATION                                                            │
│                                                                           │
│ Form:                                                                     │
```

present be	is/are/am is/are/am + not	John is in Paris. I am not on vacation.
present continuous	be + simple verb + ing be + not + simple verb + ing	Martha is flying to Canada. We are not driving.

"going to" future	be + going to + simple
	verb
	be + not + going to +
	simple verb
		The food is going to be
		    delicious.
		We are not going to eat
		    too much.

simple present	simple verb
	
	simple verb + (e)s
	
	do + not + simple verb
		I (you, we, they) take long
		    vacations.
		He (she, it) changes every
		    year.
		Joe does not like Florida.

past be	was/were was/were + not	I (he, she, it) was alone in the room. You (we, they) were so tired. She did not like the party.
simple past	simple verb + ed (many irregular) did not + simple verb	Mary liked her gift. She did not like the party.

Use:

present be	now, many times, habitual	He is always in trouble. Joe is at work now.

present continuous	now, near future	She is studying for a test
		    now.
		She is taking the test to-
		    morrow.

"going to" future	future time	We are going to California next winter.
simple present	habitual, repeated action	They often eat at restaurants. He has breakfast at 8:00 (every morning).
past be	past state or condition	Our class was late yesterday.

simple past	past completed action
	habitual, repeated action
	    in past
		I studied for one hour last night.
		We went to the library every
		    Sunday.

PRACTICE

Exercise 4: Fill in the blank with the correct form of the verb in parentheses, past, present or future.

Ex: He _*went*_ to Canada last summer. (go)

1. Peggy _____ the Eiffel Tower during her last vacation. (see)

2. Judy and John _____ to the ocean next summer. (go)

3. My brother and sister _____ next weekend. (arrive)

4. This hotel room _____ horrible! (be)

5. The strange man _____ the room two minutes ago. (leave)

6. Our friends _____ to Disney World two years ago. (go)

7. Sasha _____ a book for his next birthday. (buy)

8. My new neighbor _____ eight children and a dog. (have)

9. Abdulla and Asma _____ now. (dance)

10. The trains often _____ late this year. (come)

11. Our friend _____ a party tomorrow night. (have)

12. I _____ a ticket for last night's show. (need)

13. The children _____ fun in the amusement park yesterday. (have)

14. Lila _____ to eleven countries during her lifetime. (travel)

15. Misha _____ on the telephone with his father now. (be)

16. The president _____ at Camp David three days next week. (stay)

17. The airplane _____ very high now. (fly)

18. Joan and Bill _____ in Hong Kong in 1968. (be)

19. I _____ my aunt in Topeka now. (visit)

20. Martha _____ to work early every day. (go)

Exercise 5: Rewrite the sentences in Exercise 4. Change them to the negative form.

Ex: He went to Canada last summer.

He did not go to Canada last summer.

****

MORE PRACTICE

Exercise 6: READ AND COMMENT. Read each sentence. Write 3 more sentences to give additional information.

Ex: My friends went to a French restaurant.

A. *They ate crêpes!*

B. *They drank wine.*

C. *They got sick during dinner.*

1. Hawaii always has a lot of tourists.

    A.

    B.

    C.

2. Tom had a party last night.

    A.

    B.

    C.

3. My friend began college last month.

    A.

    B.

    C.

4. Mike and Linda bought a house last week.

    A.

    B.

    C.

5. A lot of people travel to Europe.

    A.

    B.

    C.

Exercise 7: Write a letter to your friend Jacques. He is from Paris and he wants to take a vacation. Tell him about the different possibilities below. What do most people do? Recommend a city and give Jacques some good reasons to go there.

Place	Month (Year)	Average Daily Temperature		Rainy Days
		High	Low	
Mexico City	January, 1980	70 F	41 F	5
Los Angeles	June	85	72	9
Phoenix	April, 1978	87	70	11
Honolulu	January	81	63	2
Montreal	January	21	0	17
Las Vegas	July, 1978	98	88	2
Caracas	January	75	56	6
Cairo	January, 1979	65	47	1

Begin:

Dear Jacques,
I think you should go to _____. Everybody...

Exercise 8: Describe the Shields family. Use the following information. Be as creative as you like. Here is a list of helpful phrases:

go to (a school) (a place)
work at (a company)
work as (a teacher, a secretary, etc.)
(be) promoted to (a new job)
get married
have children
take a trip (or travel)

The Shields Family

Daniel Shields (father)	Born	1927
	Education	Gateway High School, 1944 Plainville, North Dakota
	Employment	Welder, Evans Construction Company, 1945-50 Welding Supervisor, Evans Construction Company 1950-Present
	Travel	Chicago, 1948, honeymoon
Joan Bens Shields (mother)	Born	1927
	Education	Gateway High School, 1944 Mercy Nursing School, 1944-46
	Employment	Surgical Nurse, Plainville General Hospital, 1947-52 Nurse Administrator, Plainville General Hospital, 1952-54 and 1960-Present

(cont'd on next page)

| | Travel | Los Angeles, 1944 |
| | | Chicago, 1948, honeymoon |

Elizabeth May Shields (daughter)	Born	1955
	Education	Center High School, Center County, North Dakota, 1972
		University of North Dakota, 1977
	Employment	Pharmacist, Center Pharmacy, Plainville, North Dakota, 1977-Present
	Travel	Miami, 1973
		Chicago, 1975
		San Francisco, 1978
		New Orleans, 1979

COMPOSITION

Write a composition about your favorite trip.

LESSON 10   Past Continuous
             In/On/At + Place
             Place and Time Expressions

INTRODUCTION

A Frightening Experience

I was walking home from a party last night. It was very late and the streets
were empty, but I was not afraid. Nobody was on the street and the people in
my neighborhood are very nice. They often say hello and offer help. But suddenly
I was at my building, and a big man was demanding my money. His arm was around
my neck and he was holding a gun. He said, "Give me all your money. Don't make
any noise." I was very frightened. All my money was in my pocket. He was asking
for my rent and food. Here, on my street, a horrible man was mugging me.

Now I do not have any money. But this is my fault. I was walking alone
on a dark street. It was very late and my friendly neighbors were sleeping. I
was not careful. In the future, I am going to walk home with some friends. I
am not going to walk alone late at night.

GRAMMAR 1: Past Continuous

Discovery: 1. I was walking at ten o'clock.

A. What is the simple form of the first verb word? _____

    What is the simple form of the second verb word? _____

    What ending does the second verb have? _____

    What tense is the first verb? _____

GENERALIZATION

Form: past <u>be</u> + verb + <u>-ing</u>   She was eating a sandwich.

Negative = past <u>be</u> + <u>not</u> + verb +   We were not talking long.
      <u>-ing</u>.

Use: It has two basic uses.

1. It expresses an action in progress   She was reading at 10:00
    at a specific time in the past.   It was raining at 9:00 this
    The beginning and end of the action   morning.
    are not important.   I was studying for a test at
                                          7:30 last night.

2. It expresses a period of time   Everybody was arguing. Sud-
    as a background for a new   denly, I had an idea.
    action.
                                         I was walking along my street.
                                       Then I felt a gun in my ribs.

Compare simple past and past continuous.

1. Completed action vs. action in   A. Ms. Fisher wrote an ex-
    progress.   cellent article in 1975.
                                         (She completed it.)

                                         B. Ms. Fisher was writing an
                                         excellent article in 1975.
                                         (The writing was in pro-
                                         gress in 1975.)

2. Background actions and new actions.   A. The family was driving
                                         (continuous background
                                         action) to Florida. In
                                         Georgia, their car broke
                                         down. (New action)

                                         B. We were laughing and joking.
                                         (continuing background
                                         action) Suddenly, we heard
                                         a shot.
                                         (new action)

3. The verb in a <u>while</u> clause is usually   A. While the airplane was
    continuous. The second verb is   landing, a passenger pulled
    usually in the simple form.   out a gun.

                                         B. We went in the building while
                                         the men were working on it.

PRACTICE

Exercise 1: Rewrite the introduction. Change <u>I</u> to <u>you</u>. Make all necessary
             changes. (Change <u>me</u> to <u>you</u>) Begin:

You were walking home...

Exercise 2: Fill in the blank with the past continuous form of the verb in parentheses.

Ex: I _*was walking*_____ home. (walk)

1. I _____ in Chicago in 1960. (live)

2. We _____ for the test this morning. (study)

3. Muggers _____ from everybody. (steal)

4. He _____ very strange that night. (act)

5. My landlord _____ for my rent too early. (ask)

6. The thief _____ our money. (demand)

7. The children _____ in the forest. (walk)

8. That man _____ our jewelry. (take)

Exercise 3: Rewrite the sentences in Exercise 2. Change them to the negative form.

Ex: *I was not walking home.*

Exercise 4: Fill in the blank with the past continuous or simple past form of the verb in parentheses.

Bill _*was sleeping*____ at 2:00 a.m. Suddenly he _____.
    (sleep)   (awaken)

While he _____, somebody _____ into his house. Bill
          (sleep)   (break)

_____ out of bed and _____ quietly toward the stairway. He
  (get)   (walk)

_____ a heavy vase with him. While he _____, his eyes
  (take)   (walk)

_____ wide. He was trying to see the intruder. Bill walked down
  (be)

the stairs very slowly. While he _____, he _____ the vase
                                   (walk)   (carry)

high. He saw the intruder. He _____ toward the intruder. Suddenly
                                 (walk)

the intruder _____ around. He _____ Bill's son, home late.
               (turn)   (be)

GRAMMAR 2: In/On/At + Place

```
┌─────────────────────────────────────────────────────────────────────────┐
│ GENERALIZATION                                                            │
│                                                                           │
│ Use:  Use in with states, cities,        I live in Washington, D.C.       │
│       countries, and towns.              (in Oregon, in Argentina)        │
│                                                                           │
│       Use on with streets when the       He lives on Hazel Street.        │
│       house number is not given.                                          │
│                                                                           │
│       Use at with house numbers.         They live at 2771 Hazel Street.  │
└─────────────────────────────────────────────────────────────────────────┘
```

PRACTICE

Exercise 5: Fill in the blank with in, on, or at.

Ex: I live ___*on*___ Main Street.

I was visiting my aunt _____ Topeka last weekend. She lives

_____ the northern part of the city, _____ Alberta Street.

This is very interesting. I live _____ Alberta Street _____

Chicago. But we live _____ different house numbers. I live _____

2245 and my aunt lives _____ 407. Henry Caparelli, my aunt's husband,

was living with my aunt _____ 407 Alberta Street _____ Topeka.

Now he lives _____ Los Angeles.

GRAMMAR 3: Place and Time Expressions

Discovery: 1. We were walking on the street at 8:00.
            2. She was eating dinner in her room at 6:30.

Look at both sentences. Write the place phrases. 1. _____ _____ _____
                                                   2. _____ _____ _____

Write the time phrases. 1. _____ _____
                         2. _____ _____

Did we write the time and place before or after the verb? _____

Which phrase did we write first? Time or place? _____

```
┌─────────────────────────────────────────────────────────────────────────┐
│ GENERALIZATION                                                            │
│                                                                           │
│ Form:  Subject + verb + completer + place    We see our neighbors in the  │
│        + time.  Place and time expressions      store every day.          │
│        usually come after the verb.          He was visiting his friend in│
│                                                 Pittsburgh yesterday.      │
└─────────────────────────────────────────────────────────────────────────┘
```

Exercise 6: Fill in the blanks with a place and time expression. Be careful with the meaning!

Henry Caparelli is an international thief. He does a lot of "jobs" for people. For example, he stole a beautiful diamond necklace *in Paris* *two years ago* _____. He took a diamond ring _____ _____. He sold the ring _____ _____. He and his friends robbed a bank _____ _____. His friends were put in jail _____ _____ but Henry is still free.

Henry lived with his aunt _____ _____. He robbed their jewelry store _____ _____. He got some rings, watches and necklaces worth ten thousand dollars. He will sell them _____ _____.

Henry is going _____ _____. He knows about a famous diamond necklace. He will leave tomorrow. His airplane will stop _____ _____ and _____ _____. After he arrives at his destination, he will go to his hotel and prepare for his job. Henry does not want to join his friends in jail _____ _____.

****

MORE PRACTICE

Exercise 7: READ AND COMMENT. Read each sentence. Write three sentences to give additional information. Use past continuous, and time/place expressions wherever possible.

Ex: A man was watching my building this morning.

A. *He was standing across the street.*
B. *He was smoking a cigarette.*
C. *He was hiding behind a tree.*

1. A snake was sleeping near my feet.

A.

B.

C.

2. I was watching a strange man.

   A.

   B.

   C.

3. A fire was burning in my kitchen.

   A.

   B.

   C.

4. My child was choking on some candy.

   A.

   B.

   C.

5. We were driving in a snowstorm.

   A.

   B.

   C.

Exercise 8:   Write 3 paragraphs from the following outline:

Driving in a Storm

1. Family was traveling -- Whose? Where? What kind of storm? Rain? Snow? Electrical?

2. What happened? Children frightened? Parents? What were they doing?

3. How were parents helping children? Games? Sleep? Talking? What was conclusion? Happy? Sad?

Begin: ___ *family was traveling to ...*

COMPOSITION

Write a composition about a frightening experience.

LESSON 11   Questions: Yes/No, Wh-
                        Present and Past

INTRODUCTION

Request for Information

J.B. Jitendra is from Calcutta, India. He wants to study medicine after his English program. He saved some money, but he needs more. He is going to send this letter to the financial aid department of several schools.

                        Apt. 3B
                        428 Oak Street
                        Evansville, Indiana

                        March 18, 1981

Dear Sirs:

I am writing for information about financial aid for your medical program. Could you please answer some questions? What types of aid are available? I am not an American citizen. Does your school have a scholarship program for foreign students? When do I apply for these? Does the medical school offer positions as teaching assistant to foreign students? I am interested in this also. If this is not possible, do banks give low-interest loans to foreign students? Please send this information and the appropriate forms for application. Thank you very much for your help.

                        Sincerely yours,

                        J. B. Jitendra

                        J. B. Jitendra

GRAMMAR 1: Present Tense Questions: Yes/No

    Discovery: 1. Do they need something?
                2. They need information.
                3. Does he need something?
                4. He needs a scholarship.

A. Look at sentence 1 above. Is it a statement or a question? _____

    Look at sentence 2. Is it a statement or a question. _____

    What is the question word in sentence 1? _____

    Is this word simple form or -s form? _____ Why? Because the

    subject is _____

B. Look at sentence 3. Is it a statement or a question? _____

    Look at sentence 4. Is it a statement or a question? _____

85

What is the question word in sentence 3? _____ Is this word

simple form or -s form? _____ Why? Because the subject is

_____.

C. Look at <u>need</u> in 3 and 4. Which number has the -<u>s</u> form verb? _____

Which number has the simple form verb? _____

Is the main verb simple or -<u>s</u> form in questions? _____

D. Write a rule. When we write questions, we add the word _____ or _____.

Use _____ when the subject is <u>he</u>, <u>she</u>, or <u>it</u>. Use _____ when

the subject is <u>I</u>, <u>you</u>, <u>we</u>, or <u>they</u>.

Past Tense Questions: <u>Yes/No</u>

1. Did J.B. need something?
2. He needed information.
3. Did they need something?
4. They needed a scholarship.

A. Look at sentences 1 and 3 above. What is the question word in past tense

questions? _____

Are there different forms for different subjects? _____

Write a rule. Use _____ in past tense questions. It has only

_____ form.

┌───┐

GENERALIZATION

Form: <u>Do/Does</u> are the question words in simple
       present <u>yes/no</u> questions.

Use <u>do</u> when the subject is <u>I</u>, <u>you</u>, <u>we</u>   Do you want an application?
<u>they</u>, or plural.

Use <u>does</u> when the subject is <u>he</u>, <u>she</u>,   Does Martha need a job?
<u>it</u>, or singular.

Notice the main verb in questions   Does he study medicine?
is in the simple form.   Does she want a scholarship?

<u>Did</u> is the question word in simple   Did the school answer his letter?
past <u>yes/no</u> questions.   Did they write the letter?

Use <u>did</u> for all subjects. Again, the
main verb is in the simple form.

└───┘

PRACTICE

Exercise 1: Fill in the blank with <u>do</u> or <u>does</u>.

        Ex: _____*Does*_____ he live in Arizona?

1. _____ your school offer many scholarship?

2. _____ many foreign students study there?

3. _____ the professor have a lot of experience?

4. _____ the government give grants?

5. _____ the bank charge high interest rates?

6. _____ the state governments have different requirements?

7. _____ J.B. Jitendra need money?

8. _____ medical schools offer teaching positions?

9. _____ foreign students need financial assistance sometimes?

10. _____ many departments give grants?

Exercise 2: Rewrite the following sentences. Change them to yes/no questions.

Ex: He works in Mississippi.

Does he work in Mississippi ?

1. J.B. lives in Calcutta.

   _____

2. Many students apply for scholarships.

   _____

3. José and Moussa stay together on Oakland Avenue.

   _____

4. They pay a moderate rent.

   _____

5. This apartment needs a lot of work.

   _____

6. The landlord allows pets.

   _____

7. They travel to northern Spain every year.

   _____

8. The chemistry department gives some scholarships.

   _____

9. The rent includes utilities.

_____

10. Air fare costs a lot.

_____

Exercise 3:   Rewrite the following statements.   Change them to <u>yes</u>/<u>no</u> questions.

Ex: He worked in Mississippi.

Did he work in Mississippi ?

1. The city bus ran close to their apartment.

_____

2. René lived pretty far from the grocery store.

_____

3. He paid expensive utility bills last year.

_____

4. Mike saw the beautiful beaches in Chile.

_____

5. We went to the marketplace in Egypt.

_____

6. Her neighbors made a lot of noise every night.

_____

7. They had a lot of late parties during the summer.

_____

8. Marco loved the skiing in Switzerland last winter.

_____

9. Martha visited all the important sights in Paris.

_____

10. The Hermitage Museum in Leningrad impressed the tourists.

_____

GRAMMAR 2: Completer Wh- Questions

Discovery: 1. He wants something.
            2. What does he want?
            3. They want something.
            4. What do they want?

A. Look at sentence 1 above. What is the completer? _____

Look at sentence 2. What word refers to the completer? _____

What word do we use with the wh- word? _____

Why do we use <u>does</u>? Because the subject is _____

B. Look at sentence 3. What is the completer? _____

Look at sentence 4. What word refers to the completer? _____

Why do we use <u>do</u> here? Because the subject is _____

C. Look at sentences 2 and 4. Are the <u>wh-</u> words first? _____

D. Write a rule. Use <u>who</u>, <u>what</u>, <u>where</u>, and <u>when</u> to refer to the completer
    in <u>wh-</u> (information) questions. <u>Do/does</u> agrees with the _____

GENERALIZATION

Form: <u>Whom</u>, <u>what</u>, <u>where</u>, and <u>when</u>,
       can refer to the completer in
       questions.

Use <u>do</u> if the subject is <u>I</u>, <u>you</u>, <u>we</u>   Whom do they ask for information?
<u>they</u>, or plural.

Use <u>does</u> if the subject is <u>he</u>, <u>she</u>,   Where does Carlos go for help?
<u>it</u>, or singular.

NOTE: In academic or formal writing,   Whom did they ask for information?
       we usually use <u>whom</u>, not <u>who</u>.

For past tense, use <u>did</u>.   Where did Carlos go yesterday?

PRACTICE

Exercise 4: Change the following sentences to questions about the completer.

Ex: They need something.

What do they need?

1. Sabri looks at something every day.

_____

2. Despina travels somewhere in the winter.

_____

3. Carol and Ron like something.

_____

4. Ann wants something.

_____

5. Banks give loans to students sometime.

_____

6. Jorge studies somewhere every summer.

_____

7. My school has a scholarship for somebody.

_____

8. Bob and Rich go to class sometime.

_____

9. Travel agents explain their prices to somebody.

_____

10. They ask somebody for information.

_____

Exercise 5: Change the following statements to questions about the completer.

Ex: He works in Mississippi.

Where does he work?

She wanted a house.

What did she want?

1. Mohamad needed something for school last term.

_____

2. Galina lived with somebody.

_____

3. My neighbors pay somebody for help with English.

_____

4. Isao and Yikiko need something.

   _____

5. They lived somewhere.

   _____

6. Marco had an appointment at the bank sometime.

   _____

7. John and Joe went somewhere last summer.

   _____

8. Jane works in the science lab sometime.

   _____

GRAMMAR 3:   Subject Wh- Questions

   Discovery: 1.   Who needs an apartment?
                2.   John needs an apartment.
                3.   Who has scholarships?
                4.   They have scholarships.

   A.   Look at sentence 2 above. What is the subject? _____
        Look at sentence 1. What word refers to the subject? _____
        Do we use a form of do in this question type? _____

   B.   Look at sentence 4 above. What is the subject? _____
        Look at sentence 3. What word refers to the subject? _____
        Do we use a form of do in this question? _____

   C.   Look at the verbs in the questions, sentences 1 and 3. Is the verb form
        simple or the -s form? _____

   D.   Write a rule. Use who, what, where and when to refer to the subject in wh-
        questions. The verbs in present tense questions with subject wh- words are
        _____ form.

GENERALIZATION

Form:

Who, what, where, and when can also refer to the subject in questions. These questions do not use do or does. The verb is always -s form.

Who knows the finance officer?
What comes after the trip to Paris?

For past tense, the verb is in the past tense.

Who knew that man?

Compare subject with completer question forms.

Who likes the university?
(subject)(-s form)

Whom does the university admit?
(completer) (do) (subject) (simple form)

PRACTICE

Exercise 6: Change the following statements to questions about the subject.

Ex: Somebody works in Oklahoma.

Who works in Oklahoma ?

1. Somebody offers scholarships.

    _____

2. Somebody lives on Oakland Avenue.

    _____

3. Something costs a lot.

    _____

4. Somebody pays eighty dollars for utilities.

    _____

5. Somebody always pays the electric bill early.

    _____

6. Something comes in the mail every day.

    _____

7. Somebody never comes on time.

    _____

8. Something has a good variety of food.

   _____

9. Something looks beautiful.

   _____

10. Somebody knows a lot of friendly people.

   _____

Exercise 7:   Change the following statements to questions about the subject or completer.

Ex: He lived <u>in Arizona</u>.

Where did he live?

<u>J.B.</u> needs some money.

Who needs some money?

1. Something looked beautiful.

   _____

2. His school offers scholarships sometime.

   _____

3. Somebody offered a grant.

   _____

4. The landlord allows something.

   _____

5. Somebody lived in Calcutta.

   _____

6. A lot of foreign people study somewhere.

   _____

7. Something cost too much last year.

   _____

8. Something needed a lot of work.

   _____

9. He spent a lot somewhere.

   _____

10. They travel somewhere every summer.

   _____

****

MORE PRACTICE

    Exercise 10:   READ AND QUESTION. Your friend wrote the following statements to you, but he/she did not say much. Write two questions to get more information.

        Ex: We went to New York last weekend.

            A. *Did you see some plays?*
            B. *What did you do on your trip?*

1. I saw our old friends last Saturday.

   A.

   B.

2. The transportation system in this city is horrible.

   A.

   B.

3. My parents are going to China soon.

   A.

   B.

4. My brother graduated from the university last spring.

   A.

   B.

5. I am making some plans for the future.

   A.

   B.

6. I need financial assistance for the tuition this fall.

    A.

    B.

7. Our friend Charlie lives in Switzerland.

    A.

    B.

8. I am looking for a new apartment.

    A.

    B.

Exercise 11: An American friend traveled to your country last month. Write a letter to him/her. Ask about the things he saw, places he visited, and people he met. Find out if he saw the things you think are important. What did he think about your country?

COMPOSITION

Your friend in the U.S. found an apartment for you. You are going to live there while you are at the University. But your friend did not tell you much about it. Write a letter and ask your friend about the apartment, its location, its cost, its appearance, etc.

LESSON 12   Can, Will, Should

INTRODUCTION

Cultural Behavior

Every culture has a set of behavioral rules for its people. Often, the people in a culture cannot discuss these behavioral rules, but they will follow them almost every time. Unfortunately, rules of different cultures are also usually different. This can cause a lot of misunderstanding.

Consider this example. In many cultures, the people usually stand close to each other. But Americans generally stand "at arm's length" from each other. Foreign visitors should not become angry when Americans move away from them a little. But foreign visitors do not know this American rule so they become angry at the "unfriendly" Americans.

Another rule concerns eye contact. Americans look at each other but they will not look for a long time. They call this "staring" and this can seem impolite. People from many cultures show interest, respect, or friendship when they look at a person for a long time. For them, "staring" can be polite. The same behavior can cause opposite reactions in different cultures.

The foreign visitor will not be able to learn all the rules of a new culture. But he should be patient in the new culture. He will often be angry, confused, or frustrated. Before he says or does anything in these situations, he should consider the possibility of cultural differences.

GRAMMAR: Can, Will, Should

    Discovery: 1. The same behavior can cause opposite results.
                2. People will follow their cultural rules
                3. Foreign visitors should be patient.

    A. Look at sentences 1, 2, and 3. List the subjects. _____, _____, _____.
    B. List the verbs. _____, _____, _____.
    C. Look at the first word in each verb group. Are there any -s forms? _____
    D. Look at the second word in each verb group. Are there any -s forms? _____
    E. Write a rule. Use can, will, and should with another _____.
        The verbs do not have the _____ form.

96

GENERALIZATION

Form:
$\left.\begin{matrix} \underline{can} \\ \underline{will} \\ \underline{should} \end{matrix}\right\}$ + simple verb

Foreign visitors should be patient.

These verbs never have an -s form

Differences can cause problems.
Visitors will make mistakes.
They should consider behavioral rules.

NOTE: We do not write to between the modal (can, will, should) and the simple verb.

Negative:

$\left.\begin{matrix} \underline{can} \\ \underline{will} \\ \underline{should} \end{matrix}\right\}$ + not + simple verb.

Visitors should not be angry.
They cannot learn all the rules.
(Notice cannot is one word).

Use: can = ability

I can speak English, but I cannot speak German.

will = future (promise, determination, or inevitability)

He will do it tomorrow. (promise)
We will drive until we arrive.
                    (determination)
The lecture will probably be long.
                    (inevitability)

should = be a good idea, advice

Americans should be more friendly.

Present or future time words can be used with can and should but never past time words.

They should come now/tomorrow.
They can eat at home now/tomorrow.

Frequency adverbs come after models.

He can always ask the teacher.
You should never stare at Americans.
Americans will sometimes hide their feelings.
Visitors should always be patient.

PRACTICE

Exercise 1: Rewrite the following sentences to show "it is a good idea."

Ex: He studies English.

He should study English.

1. John smiles a lot.

   _____

2. People remain quiet in the elevators.

   _____

3. Everybody says, "Fine, thank you."

   _____

4. My friend always shakes my hand.

   _____

5. Tourists and students learn something about foreign cultures.

   _____

Exercise 2:   Rewrite the following sentences to show "ability."

   Ex: They speak English.

   They can speak English.

1. Cultural differences cause misunderstandings.

   _____

2. We study cultural differences today.

   _____

3. We ask friends for help with cultural problems.

   _____

4. A scientist describes these differences.

   _____

5. Teasing often makes people uncomfortable.

   _____

Exercise 3:   Rewrite the following statements to show "promise, determination, or inevitability."

   Ex: They study Chinese.

   They will study Chinese.

1. Women get angry about "staring."

   _____

2. An American is always "Fine."

   _____

3. They say "Hi" too often.

   _____

4. My American friend often asks his teacher for help.

   _____

5. Americans are always serious about time.

   _____

   Exercise 4: Rewrite the following sentences. Change them to the negative form.

   Ex: They can study English.

   They cannot study English.

1. Late students should sit down quietly.

   _____

2. Ernesto will write a thesis about cultural differences.

   _____

3. Scientists can study cultural differences.

   _____

4. Foreign visitors should be patient in different countries.

   _____

5. Women can work in the same jobs as men.

   _____

6. A tourist will have problems in the new country.

   _____

7. Students should ask their teachers about cultural rules.

   _____

8. Americans will always be serious about time.

   _____

9. American tourists should study differences in other countries.

   _____

10. Teachers can help foreign students with cultural problems.

    _____

Exercise 5: Read the situation and fill in the blank with <u>can</u>, <u>will</u>, or <u>should</u> according to the meaning in parentheses.

Ex: John is going to be a doctor. (good idea)

He _*should*_ study hard.

1. Jack is standing on the elevator. (good idea)

   He _____ look toward the doors.

2. Kitty is a linguist. (ability)

   She _____ speak three foreign languages.

3. Chen needs advice about school. (good idea)

   He _____ ask his teacher or advisor.

4. Ali is interested in tourism. (determination)

   He _____ major in travel management.

5. Men and women in the U.S. are equal. (ability)

   Women _____ work in any job.

6. Many people do not understand cultural differences. (inevitability)

   They _____ often become angry.

7. My friend and I had some cultural problems. (promise not to do something)

   In the future, I _____ stare and he _____ move away.

8. Marco is late for class. (not a good idea)

   He _____ talk to the teacher immediately.

9. Many people shake hands during an introduction. (good idea)

   The handshake _____ always be firm.

10. Americans enjoy teasing people. (ability)

    These jokes _____ make people comfortable or uncomfortable.

11. Sonia hates the dinner at her friend's house. (ability)

    She _____ say she is not very hungry.

12. Michael got a horrible haircut. (determination not to do something)

    His friend _____ say it is horrible.

13. José is on an empty bus downtown. (inevitable something does not happen)

    The people probably _____ sit near him.

14. The American culture is different. (inability)

    Foreign students _____ understand it immediately.

15. The American culture is actually many cultures. (inevitability)

    People in one part of the country _____ be different from people in other parts.

****

MORE PRACTICE

   Exercise 6: Read the following situations and write three possible statements as advice, ability and inevitability (promise or determination).

   Ex: Americans stand "at arm's length."
   A. *I should understand this rule.*
   B. *I can stand at arm's length.*
   C. *They will not usually stand close to each other.*

1. Many American classes are informal.

   A.

   B.

   C.

2. Americans do not stand close to people.

   A.

   B.

   C.

3. My friend thinks Americans smile too much.

   A.

   B.

   C.

4. American people always say "Fine, thank you."

   A.

   B.

   C.

5. Americans love to joke and tease.

   A.

   B.

   C.

   Exercise 7: Write a composition using the following guidelines. The subject is cheating.

   Cheating is help during a test or with homework without the teacher's permission.

1. In your country:

   Explain the rules the people in your country have. What should a student do if he does not understand? Can students talk during a test? Can they help other students? What will the teacher do if the student breaks the rules? (angry? lower grade? take the paper?)

2. In the U.S.:

   Is cheating permitted in the U.S.? Did you understand American classroom rules at first? What are these rules? What mistakes did you or your friends make about cheating?

COMPOSITION

   A good friend from your country is going to study in the U.S. Write a letter to him. Explain the cultural differences he will need to know.

LESSON 13   Completer Pronouns
            Articles

INTRODUCTION

Traffic Laws in the U.S.

Each state in the U.S. has a set of traffic laws. Every driver must obey them.
These laws are similar from state to state, but they are not always the same.

Pennsylvania has a lot of laws about parking, turning, accidents, and insurance.
For example, a driver should not park his car beside another car. He should park
it on the side of the street or in a space for parking. If the driver has an
accident, he must immediately stop his car and ask the other driver for his address
and insurance company and give this information to him also. Every driver must
have insurance for his car. If the accident caused more than one hundred dollars'
damage, the drivers should report it to the Department of Transportation within
three days. Drivers can also turn right when the traffic light is red. But they
must stop first.

When a driver makes a mistake and breaks a traffic law, a policeman will usually
give him a ticket. The driver will pay a fine. However, if the driver has an
accident and does not stop, he can go to jail and lose his license.

GRAMMAR 1: Completer Pronouns

Discovery: 1. The policeman remembered the nervous driver.
            2. He remembered him.

A. Compare the two examples above. What does <u>he</u> refer to in sentence 2?
    _____ him? _____

B. Can we use adjectives or <u>a/the</u> with completer pronouns (<u>him</u>)? _____

```
GENERALIZATION

Form:

    Subject Pronouns      Completer Pronouns

          I                    me
        you                   you
         we                    us            John drove too fast.
        they                  them           The policeman caught him
         he                   him              and wrote a ticket.
        she                   her            He paid it at court.
         it                    it

Use:

We use completer pronouns to avoid        Martha bought a small car.
repetitions.                              She likes it a lot.

Notice, we cannot describe a completer    John saw the horrible accident.
pronoun with adjectives or articles.  We  He described it to his friends.
replace the whole noun phrase.
```

PRACTICE

Exercise 1: Fill in the blank with the correct completer pronoun, according to the first sentence.

Ex: John saw the horrible accident.

He described *it* to his friends.

1. Traffic laws in the U.S. are different.

   José is going to study _____ before he drives.

2. Marget had an accident with Ali.

   She talked to _____ immediately.

3. Jian Yi said, "Thank you for your help with my driving test.

   I'll help _____ some day, too."

4. Misha had an accident with an elderly woman.

   He helped _____ immediately.

5. In Pennsylvania, pedestrians have the "right of way."

   Drivers stop for _____ .

6. Jenny paid a fine for speeding yesterday.

   She paid _____ by mail.

7. We were in a big train accident.

   Luckily, it did not hurt _____ .

8. John had an accident a few minutes ago.

   He will report _____ tomorrow.

9. We heard a police car late last night.

   We saw _____ later.

10. Somebody stole my car last night.

    The policemen asked _____ about it.

Exercise 2: Rewrite the sentences. Replace the underlined words with a completer pronoun or a subject pronoun.

Ex: John and Jack are in jail.

They are in jail. .

1. Al Capone committed a lot of crimes in the 1930's.
2. Charlie stole the diamond ring.
3. Khatib trepassed on private property.
4. Somebody stole Tarik's new car.
5. Jane bought insurance for her children.
6. People should not park near an intersection.
7. The men wanted their neighbor to be quiet.
8. Karen should report her lost license to the authorities.
9. Cindy drove 65 miles per hour in a 55 mile zone.
10. Joe left the accident immediately.
11. The police found the criminals in an empty building.
12. John saw the accident and described it to the police.
13. The thief lied to the judge.
14. Mrs. James will testify in court tomorrow.
15. The police helped the woman after the explosion.

GRAMMAR 2: Articles The/A

GENERALIZATION

Form: The English articles are the and a/an.

She saw the collision.
She saw a collision.

We write a before words which begin with a consonant sound.

a car
a law
a unique car (the first sound is [y])

Write an before words which begin with a vowel sound.

an insurance form
an hour (the first sound is [a])

GENERALIZATION CONTINUED ON THE NEXT PAGE

GENERALIZATION

Use:

Use the with singular or plural, count, or non-count nouns.	the law, the laws the advice
Use a/an with singular, count nouns only.	an experience, a law
Use the with previously mentioned nouns. Use a with new information.	John had an accident. The accident was not bad.

PRACTICE

Exercise 3: Fill in the blanks with a/an or the.

Ex: I need ___the___ information.

1. My neighbor gave me _____ sugar.

2. Mark knows _____ policemen on the police force.

3. _____ new cars drive very fast.

4. Nadja reported _____ news last night.

5. We voted for _____ new laws.

6. He wants _____ information soon.

7. They have _____ knowledge but they do not have any experience.

8. I gave him_____ advice and left.

9. They passed _____ laws in Alaska.

10. Their driving teacher gave _____ students a driving test.

Exercise 4: Fill in the blank with a, the or X according to the situation.

Ex: We had ___a___ test yesterday.
Saleh cheated on ___the___ test.

1. Jane loves _____ cars.

She bought _____ Volvo yesterday.

2. Massa's parents are going to visit her.

_____ visit will be short.

3. Tomoko is _____ very good driver.

   She is going to take _____ trip tomorrow.

4. Chen is going to watch _____ trial.

   _____ trial is tomorrow afternoon.

5. We saw _____ accident yesterday.

   _____ accident was very bad.

6. Everybody likes the new law about right turns.

   It is _____ big help to drivers.

7. The world has a lot of countries.

   Each one has _____ set of laws.

8. Mira does not always tell the truth.

   Yesterday, she told _____ big lie.

9. Ken has _____ new car.

   It has two doors and _____ large trunk.

10. Policemen wear uniforms during the work day.

    _____ uniforms are black.

11. We parked on _____ side street.

    _____ street was narrow and short.

12. Bob got _____ ticket for speeding.

    _____ ticket cost him 25 dollars.

****

MORE PRACTICE

Exercise 5: READ AND COMMENT. Read each sentence and write 3 more sentences to give additional information. Use completer pronouns when possible. Be careful with a/an and the.

Ex: I live in an apartment.

A. *The apartment is very nice.*

B. *I like it very much.*

C. *My new neighbors are friendly.*

1. I am going to buy a new car.

   A.

   B.

   C.

2. John hit a young girl with his car.

   A.

   B.

   C.

3. Şükriye got a ticket for driving without her license.

   A.

   B.

   C.

4. My country has a lot of traffic laws.

   A.

   B.

   C.

5. Sarah was a witness at a two-car accident.

   A.

   B.

   C.

Exercise 6: Write a short composition about driver training in your country. Use the following outline:

1. How old is a person before he can drive? How does he learn? (classroom, friends, family?) Is there a lot to study?

2. Do people get licenses? Do they take driving tests? Do you have a license? Describe the test.

3. Which country has better drivers, the U.S. or your country? Why? (too fast, careful?

Begin: *In my country, a person can drive when...*

COMPOSITION

Write a composition about the laws in your country in one of the following areas:

A. Traffic

B. Criminal

C. (the area of your choice, but ask your teacher)

LESSON 14   Other/Another
              Possessive Nouns

INTRODUCTION

"Progress"

We hear a lot about progress today. One person says factories are producing
a lot of wonderful products. Another says they are producing a lot of pollution.
One person praises modern television's informative role. Others blame television
for children's poor education, sexual promiscuity,and murder in the streets.

Everything is changing very quickly these days. Our children can come from
test tubes and we can predict their sex. We have wonderful, high-speed cars. Space
travel is almost easy now. We are very comfortable people, for now.

But some people are not very comfortable. Earthquakes, floods, tornadoes,
volcanoes, and droughts destroy people and property. People die every day from
incurable diseases. A lot of people in our world do not have any food or medicine.
These people do not worry about television, production, or cars. They have other
worries. In short, our "progress" is very strong in some areas and very weak in
others.

GRAMMAR 1: Other/Another

Discovery:

Adjectives   1. I read this article about pollution, but Jane read the other
                  one.
              2. Mary saw these new bridges, but John saw the other ones.
              3. He wrote one letter to the congressman, then he wrote
                  another one.
              4. The congressman talked to some people, but he missed other ones.

A. Look at the sentences above. Which "other" adjectives are used with

    singular nouns? _____

    Which ones are used with plural nouns? _____

110

Pronouns: 1. I read this article, but Jane read <u>the other</u>.
           2. Mary saw these bridges, but John saw <u>the others</u>.
           3. He wrote one letter, then he wrote <u>another</u>.
           4. The congressman talked to some people, but he missed <u>others</u>.

B. Look at the sentences above. The "other" adjectives are pronouns now.

What are the singular pronouns? _____

What are the plural pronouns? _____

GENERALIZATION

Form:

	Definite	Indefinite
<u>Singular</u>	the other one the other	another one another
<u>Plural</u>	the other ones the others	other ones others

Use:

<u>(The) other(s)/another</u> mean "a different object" in the subject or completer. We always use them after a previous mention of the object (often with <u>one/ones</u>).

I like this movie, but the other one was horrible.

Use the <u>other + noun</u> or <u>the other(s)</u> when you are writing about a specific thing/things or person/people (definite).

He reviewed the new science journal, but he forgot the other ones.

Use <u>another + noun</u> or other(s) when you are writing about a non-specific or general thing/things or person/people (indefinite).

He reviewed some journals, but he forgot other ones.

PRACTICE

Exercise 1: Read each sentence. Write a second sentence in the negative using <u>other</u>. Use the information from the first sentence in the second one, too.

Ex: Some people like television.

Other people do not like television.

1. Some students study a lot.

2. Some people like nuclear power.

3. Some people believe in God.

4. Some families have a lot of money.

5. Some people will live in space.

6. Some animals can understand English.

7. Some babies begin in test tubes.

8. Some industrial cities have a lot of air pollution.

9. Some governments have laws against pollution.

10. Some books are fun to read.

Exercise 2: Read each sentence. Write a second sentence in the negative using
another. Use the information from the first sentence in the second
sentence, too.

Ex: One man needs warm weather.

Another man does not need warm weather.

1. One earthquake causes a lot of damage.

2. One person is healthy and happy.

3. One new television show is for the family.

4. One busy man loves his family.

5. One person walks to work.

6. One modern machine helps mankind.

7. One hard-working scientist is developing medicine.

8. One building is very modern.

9. One working woman earns a lot of money.

10. One family has a lot of children.

Exercise 3: Read each sentence. Write a second sentence in the negative using
the other. Use the information from the first sentence in your
second sentence, too.

Ex: These men are tired.

The other men are not tired.

1. These cars are very modern.

2. This spaceship travels very fast.

3. This book is complicated.

4. This Swiss watch is expensive.

5. These women want equal rights.

6. This new fuel is difficult to find.

7. These storms are very severe.

8. These young men are going to war.

9. This earthquake killed a lot of people.

10. These television shows are disgusting.

Exercise 4: Rewrite your sentences in Exercise 1. Change the adjective <u>other</u> to the pronoun form <u>the other</u> or <u>others</u>.

Ex: Other people do not like television.

Others do not like television

Exercise 5: Rewrite <u>your</u> sentences in Exercise 2. Change the adjective <u>another</u> to the pronoun <u>another</u>.

Ex: Another man does not need warm weather.

Another does not need warm weather.

Exercise 6: Rewrite <u>your</u> sentences in Exercise 3. Change the adjective <u>the other</u> to the pronoun the <u>other(s)</u>.

Ex: The other men are not tired.

The others are not tired

Exercise 7: Read each opinion. Write a second, changed opinion according to the cue. Use the cue and <u>(the) other(s)/another</u> in your answer. Use the pronoun form in opinions with an asterisk (*).

Ex: Nuclear power plants are dangerous. (some)

Some nuclear power plants are dangerous but other nuclear power plants are safe.

Ex: *People are worried about the future. (one)

One person is worried about the future but another is not.

1. Earthquakes kill people. (some)

*2. The young men went to war. (these)

3. The city is modern. (one)

*4. Our hospital has modern equipment. (this)

5. Americans like solar energy. (some)

*6. A student in my building is going to be a doctor. (one)

7. The areas around the factory are polluted. (some)

*8. A woman in my class is going to have a baby. (one)

9. The movie on TV now is great. (this)

10. TV programs can be very instructive. (these)

11. The scientific discovery was very good. (one)

*12. Long books are easy to read. (some)

13. A doctor can often cure diseases. (one)

*14. Scientists are very intelligent. (some)

15. An American woman has a lot of opportunities. (this)

GRAMMAR 2: Possessive Nouns

Discovery: 's/' form

        1. It is the man's report.
        2. That was the scientists' statement.

A. Look at the two statements. Are man's and scientists' adjectives, nouns, or verbs? _____
    Is man singular or plural? _____ scientists'? _____

B. Man's and scientists' are possessive forms. What is the possessive ending for man? _____ for scientists? _____
    Does it change from singular to plural? _____
    Singular is _____. Plural is _____.

C. Write a rule. Add _____ to the end of singular nouns to form the possessive. Add _____ to the end of plural nouns.

GENERALIZATION

Form:

Add 's to the possessor noun when it is singular. Add ' when it is plural.

The girl has a red dress.
The girl's red dress is beautiful.
The students have a lot of homework.
The students' homework is difficult.

NOTE: people   people's
       men   men's
       women   women's

Do not add 's or ' to pronouns. Remember, they have special possessive forms. (see Lesson 5).

She has a red dress.
Her red dress is beautiful.

Use:

Use this form with animate nouns to show possession.

Discovery: of form

1. The cover of the book is red.
2. The colors of the lamp are beautiful.

A. Look at the sentences above. What word did we use to show possession here? _____

GENERALIZATION

Form: An alternate possessive form is noun + of + (a/the/etc.) + noun

The color of her hair is black.

Use: We usually use this form with inanimate nouns.

The end of the movie was wonderful.

PRACTICE

Exercise 8: Make a sentence from each item. Use possessive forms and the verb be.

Ex: men/liberation/a current issue

Men's liberation is a current issue.

1. The professor/speech/about astronomy

2. a child/education/very important

3. the scientist/experiment/almost complete

4. women/rights/an important issue/in 1930

5. the reporter/story/on the 6:00 news/last night

6. people/welfare/an important concern

7. an astronomer/discoveries/very exciting

8. the students/projects/finished next month

9. one person/progress/another person/horror

10. a person/television/his companion

Exercise 9: Rewrite each sentence to show possession with '_s_ or '. The verb will always be a form of _be_.

Ex: Jane has a daughter in school.

Jane's daughter is in school.

Ex: Mrs. Smith bought a big house.

Mrs. Smith's house is big.

1. The coats in the closet belong to the boys.

2. Mrs. Johnson has a dog in her apartment.

3. Scientists make important discoveries.

4. That book on the table belongs to the teacher.

5. The assignment about Chile belongs to Alejandra.

6. Janet has a brother in Alaska.

7. Giancarlo owned a car in Venezuela.

8. The geologist has very sensitive instruments.

9. A chemist conducts complex experiments.

10. The students gave a speech about progress.

11. The other professor offers interesting courses.

12. My wife has an extremely handsome husband!

13. Teachers have a lot of responsibility in the classroom.

14. The boss made a speech about water pollution.

Exercise 10: Rewrite the following sentences to show possession with <u>of</u>.

Ex: The world's wars killed a lot of people.

The wars of the world killed a lot of people.

1. Women's liberation is causing a lot of social changes.

2. The companies' opinions were disgraceful.

3. The country's pollution problems are growing.

4. China's political system is interesting.

5. Nuclear power's dangers are great.

6. The earthquakes' effects will last a long time.

7. Movies' themes are often childish.

8. Houses' designs are small and simple now.

9. Science's progress is important to mankind.

10. Many people discuss television's dangers.

****

MORE PRACTICE

Exercise 11: READ AND COMMENT. Read each sentence. Write 2 more sentences as additional information. Use the possessive and <u>other/another</u> when possible.

Ex: Some people like nuclear power.

A. *Other people hate it.*
B. *Young children's parents think it is dangerous.*

1. Television is very popular in the U.S.

A.

B.

2. Some people think test tube babies are an immoral idea.

A.

B.

3. People have different opinions about air pollution.

   A.

   B.

4. Some people think the 21st century will be very exciting.

   A.

   B.

5. People's ideas of progress vary.

   A.

   B.

Exercise 12: Write a composition about the "Dangers of Television" according to the following outline. Compare people's opinions, good (pro) and bad (con). Include your opinions also. Use some "other" adjectives and pronouns and possessive nouns.

Begin: *Some people think that television is ...*

Pro	Con
1. helps students' creativity	1. makes students lazy
2. educates	2. people's minds get dull from TV
3. shows children reality	3. shows children too many bad things (violence, sex, crime)
4. teaches about the real world in a real way	4. hero's images are false
5. provokes thought about new experiences	5. it's an idiot box; people do not think during programs
6. many programs are very good	6. the quality of programs is very poor

COMPOSITION

Write a composition about one of the following topics. Compare your opinions with other people's opinions.

A. The 21st Century
B. Women's Liberation
C. Test Tube Babies

LESSON 15   Past <u>Going to</u>
            Prearticles/Count and Non-Count

INTRODUCTION

The Tale of Kinderfella

Fairy tales are popular traditional stories about kings and queens, beautiful girls and handsome men, or horrible people or monsters. Fairy tales are popular in most of the world and especially in the U.S. One of the most popular fairy tales is <u>Cinderella</u>. It is the story of a beautiful girl and her horrible stepmother. Below is the story of <u>Kinderfella</u>, Cinderella's relative.

Kinderfella was born in the wrong fairy tale. Most of the men in his story were handsome princes. But Kinderfella was ugly and big-nosed. His parents were going to leave him at the beginning of the story. They were going to continue the fairy tale without him. Of course, this did not happen, but it almost did.

Most of the people in Kinderfella's village did not usually talk to him, but one day, some of his neighbors felt sorry for him. They told him about a big party for the King that night.

"Can I go?" Kinderfella asked. "Well," answered one neighbor, "The King won't invite you but the old lady at 2217 can help. Talk to her. "

Kinderfella was excited and went to the old lady immediately. "Well," she answered, "Put this pill in your mouth at midnight to-night and you will go to the party. That'll be ten dollars please."

That night, Kinderfella stared at his watch until midnight. He was so excited. He put the pill in his mouth at midnight and waited. Suddenly, he felt strange. He felt very strange. He went to the mirror and looked. Oh no! He was a horse! An ugly horse, of course. He was going to be a handsome prince! Instead, he'll only carry handsome dancers to the party -- on his back!

GRAMMAR 1: Past <u>Going to</u>

Discovery: 1. He was going to visit us. But he did not.
             2. They were going to talk to her. Instead,
                 they'll write.

A.   Look at sentences 1 and 2. Is the action <u>completed</u> or <u>considered</u>? _____

B.   Which verb form do we use to show considered action? Past _____ +

_____ + _____

```
GENERALIZATION

Form:  Past going to =

       was ⎱
       were ⎰ + going to + simple verb    The child was going to leave.

   Negative =

   was ⎱
   were ⎰ + not going to + simple verb    He was not going to stay.

   Use:  Past going to shows action which    The girl was going to cry.
         was considered but not completed.      (She didn't.)
                                              The children were going to sing.
                                                 (They didn't.)


   Compare past going to with simple past.   The prince was going to dance,
                                                but he sang instead.
                                              The prince danced and enjoyed
                                                 it very much.
```

PRACTICE

Exercise 1: Fill in the blank with the correct form of past going to and the
             verb in parentheses.

Ex: The children _were going to ride_____ on the magic carpet.
                        (ride)

1. The good fairy _____ them. (help)

2. We _____ to Oz. (travel)

3. The children _____ lost in the forest. (get)

4. Snow White _____ forever. (sleep)

5. He _____ the magic words. (say)

6. The dwarfs _____ the old witch. (kill)

7. The neighbors _____ the lost child. (help)

8. The witch _____ the children. (hurt)

9. The young girl's hair _____ for a hundred years. (grow)

10. The old lady _____ a special medicine. (make)

Exercise 2: Rewrite the sentences above. Change them to the <u>negative</u> form.

Ex: The children were going to ride on the magic carpet.

The children were not going to ride on the magic carpet.

Exercise 3: Read each sentence below. Write a sentence to explain if the action was completed or only considered.

Ex: I was going to go to Chicago. *I did not.*

I went to Chicago. *I did.*

They were not going to write that. *They did.*

1. The frog was going to marry a prince. _____

2. The King had a party. _____

3. Kinderfella's neighbors were not going to talk to him. _____

4. The monster was going to eat the children. _____

5. The wolf ate the grandmother. _____

6. The little man was going to steal the magic lamp. _____

7. The children were not going to talk to the witch. _____

8. The grandmother did not see the wolf. _____

9. The sky was going to fall. _____

10. Kinderfella went to the old lady. _____

11. The old lady was going to help him. _____

12. The girl did not go to the Wizard of Oz. _____

13. Kinderfella's parents were going to leave him. _____

14. The beautiful girl said Rumpelstiltskin's name. _____

15. The stepmother was not going to help Cinderella. _____

GRAMMAR 2:   Prearticles With Count and Non-count Nouns:

Discovery: 1. <u>All of</u> the people know him.
               2. <u>Some of</u> their children hate him.
               3. He has <u>most of</u> their money.
               4. <u>None of</u> their parents like him.
               5. He does not like <u>any of</u> the parents.

A. Look at the sentences above. What word follows <u>all</u>, <u>some</u>, <u>most</u>, and <u>none</u>?

_____

B. What kinds of nouns can follow these words? _____ and _____

C. Do we usually use <u>none of</u> in the completer? _____ What do we

    usually use instead of <u>none of</u>?   _____

GENERALIZATION

Form: <u>all</u>
        <u>most</u>   } + <u>of</u> + (<u>noun phrase</u> (NP)
        <u>some</u>   the + noun   the people
        <u>none/any</u>)   possessive + noun   my friends
                                         demonstrative + noun those stories

The noun phrase (NP) can have   All of the stories are good.
count or non-count nouns.   None of the money will be ours.
                                      They took some of the candy.
                                      Most of the boys were going to cry.

Notice count nouns are plural.   Some of the women were beautiful.
Remember non-count nouns do   None of the information was important.
  not change form.   He knows most of the people.

We usually use <u>none of</u> in the None of the information was valuable.
  subject, but <u>any of</u> in the   Did you see any of the people?
  completer.   We did not see any of the people.

Use: <u>All of</u>, <u>some of</u>, <u>most of</u>,
      and <u>none of</u> tell how many
      things or people of a group.

Compare: Some people like fairy tales.
                                      Some of the people (in my country)
                                        like them.

PRACTICE

Exercise 4: Fill in the blank with the correct present tense form of the verb in parentheses.

Ex: Most of the people ___*are*___ in China. (be)

None of the advice ___*is*___ good. (be)

1. Most of the music from the forest _____ beautiful. (be)

2. Some of the prince's suggestions _____ intelligent. (be)

3. None of the village people _____ in the forest. (live)

4. Most of the people's ideas _____ good. (be)

5. The King _____ most of the orders in his kingdom. (give)

6. Some of the children _____ lost in the forest. (be)

7. People _____ to advice some of the time, but not all. (listen)

8. All of the men _____ the princess. (love)

9. None of the poison _____ on her lips. (remain)

10. Most of the women in our country _____ colorful clothes. (wear)

Exercise 5: Fill in the blank with the correct form of the noun in parentheses.

Ex: Most of the ___*information*___ came from the witch.
(information)

Most of the ___*stories*___ are interesting. (story)

1. Most of the _____ were frightened of the witches. (villager)

2. Some of the witch's _____ was harmful. (advice)

3. None of the _____ she gave was good. (help)

4. The children ate some of the _____ in the little house. (sugar)

5. Most of the _____ helped the old woman. (man)

6. All of the _____ held little monsters. (eggs)

7. The frightened children heard some of the good fairy's _____. (music)

8. They were afraid most of the _____. (time)

9. All of the _____ in fairy tales are beautiful.
(princess)

10. The children did not drink any of the poisoned _____.
(water)

Exercise 6: Rewrite the sentences below using all of, most of, some of, or none of according to the word in parentheses. Change the underlined part of the sentence.

Ex: A child likes fairy tales. (some)

Some of the children like fairy tales.

1. Children in the U.S. read fairy tales. (most)

2. The old woman was cruel. (all)

3. German fairy tales are popular in the U.S. (some)

4. The child was lost and afraid. (most)

5. The thieves were waiting for the King. (all)

6. Our trip was very long. (some)

7. They obeyed the laws. (none)

8. The bad people went to jail. (some)

9. The children were orphans. (all)

10. The houses had a lot of laughter. (none)

****

MORE PRACTICE

Exercise 8: Answer the following questions truthfully. Use all of, most of, some of, or none of in your answers.

Ex: Do you like fairy tales?

I like some of the fairy tales.

1. Do people in your country read fairy tales?

2. Do the people in your country like wars?

3. Do you always like the weather?

4. What do your friends like to do?

5. Where are your friends now?

6. Is your family with you now?

7. Do students sleep all night?

8. Do students study a lot?

9. Where do you keep your money?

10. Where do you buy your food?

11. Where do you spend your free time?

12. When do you do your homework?

Exercise 9: READ AND COMMENT. Read each sentence and write three more sentences as additional information. Use past <u>going to</u> and prearticles when possible.

Ex: I was going to marry a prince.

A. *Most of my friends laughed at this dream.*
B. *I considered the handsome men here.*
C. *I married a frog instead.*

1. The old witch was going to kidnap the children.

A.

B.

C.

2. The children were lost in a magical country.

A.

B.

C.

3. The lady was beautiful during the day but ugly at night.

A.

B.

C.

4. A monster was eating all the travelers.

    A.

    B.

    C.

5. The animals were talking about a strange event.

    A.

    B.

    C.

    Exercise 10:   Read the following outline, then write the story of <u>Cinderella</u>. Be as creative as you like. Describe all the parts. Use past <u>going to</u> and prearticles when possible.

1. Her father married a cruel woman with two cruel sisters. Then he died.

2. She did all of the work for her family.

3. The King was having a ball (party). Cinderella wanted to go.

4. Her fairy godmother helped her.

5. She went to the ball. The prince loved her. Describe the ball.

6. What happened next?

   Begin: *Cinderella lived in a small kingdom many years ago. Her mother died when she was young so her father ...*

COMPOSITION

Tell the story of your favorite (or your country's favorite) fairy tale.

    -or-

Create your own fairy tale.

LESSON 16   <u>Ought to</u>, <u>Might</u>, <u>Have to</u>
            <u>Prearticles</u> (Count and Non-count Nouns)

INTRODUCTION

<u>Marriage and Dating</u>

American dating customs are changing. In the old days, many of the young
people met their future partners in their parents' homes. Nowadays, there are more
possibilities. They might meet people at work or at school. They might meet them
at church or through another organization. But the really different meeting place
is the single's bar.* People in single's bars have to like loud music, because
much of the time, they will dance or listen to it. They have to drink a little,
smile a lot, and have fun. Of course, this is not very hard.

Some of the single's bars have interesting "gimmicks."** Many of them have
a lot of plants, antiques, or other special decorations. A few of them have in-house
telephones on every table. People call the people they like. A few of the others
use computers and give each person a popularity score. All of the "gimmicks"
increase the fun.

The next time you want to meet people and have fun, you ought to try a single's
bar. Try the popular ones with the biggest crowds.

* A single's bar is a bar where unmarried people can meet each other.
** A "gimmick" is a special thing that causes more interest in the place.

GRAMMAR 1:   Prearticles (With Count and Non-count Nouns)

Discovery: 1.   <u>Many of the people</u> like singles bars.
              2.   They dance and listen to music <u>much of the time</u>.
              3.   <u>A few of the bars</u> have "gimmicks."
              4.   <u>A little of the fun</u> comes from the "gimmicks."

A. What word always follows <u>many</u>, <u>much</u>, <u>a few</u>, and <u>a little</u> in the sentences
    above? _____

B. Which two phrases take count nouns? _____ and _____.

C. Which two phrases take non-count nouns? _____ and _____.

D. Are the count nouns in these phrases plural? _____
    Are the non-count ones plural? _____

127

```
GENERALIZATION

Form:


much   }  + of +  (non-count noun phrase (NP)
a little }          (the + singular noun              the time
                        possessive + singular noun    his homework
                     (demonstrative + singular noun   that music


many  }    + of +  (count noun phrase (NP)
a few }            (the + plural noun                 the bars
                    possessive + plural noun          his friends
                    demonstrative + plural noun       those gimmicks
                   (completer pronoun                 them, us, you
```

NOTICE: It is possible to use completer   some of us . . .
          pronouns with all prearticles   None of them . . .
          that can take count nouns. Do not   Many of you . . .
          use subject pronouns with them.   Most of us . . .

Use:

Much of, many of, a little of, and   Saad went to a few of the bars.
a few of tell how many things or   Much of the music was terrible.
people from a group.   (Not all)

PRACTICE

Exercise 1: Fill in the blank with the correct form of the noun in parentheses.

Ex: Many of the single's _*bars*_____ have "gimmicks." (bar)

1. Many of the young _____ like single's bars. (adult)

2. We liked a few of the _____ we met. (person)

3. A little of the _____ spoiled during the party. (food)

4. Jane met many of those _____ at church. (man)

5. We spent much of our _____ at the party. (time)

6. We liked a little of their _____, but not all of it. (music)

7. Do you know many of my _____? (friend)

8. Much of the _____ he gave was bad. (advice)

9. Mike spent a little of his _____ on a girl. (money)

10. A few of Jack's _____ work at his company. (friend)

Exercise 2: Rewrite the following sentences. Change the underlined word or phrase to a prearticle (<u>much/many of</u>, <u>a few/little of</u>) + NP. Be sure to use examples of each.

You must choose the correct prearticle from each pair.

Ex: <u>Adults</u> like singles bars.

Many of the adults like singles' bars.

<u>Singles' bars</u> have "gimmicks."

A few of the singles' bars have "gimmicks."

1. <u>People</u> meet other people in a variety of ways.

2. <u>A young person</u> dates when he is thirteen or fourteen.

3. Joe spent his <u>money</u> on his girlfriend.

4. The <u>advice</u> my friend gave was very good.

5. <u>Engagements</u> for marriage can be very long.

6. <u>A wedding</u> is elaborate.

7. <u>The dance</u> was a lot of fun, but noisy.

8. The <u>music</u> at her wedding was classical.

9. Jane met <u>her friends</u> at the laundromat.

10. Gary took his <u>girlfriend</u> to the movies.

Exercise 3: Read the following statements. Write a sentence to show agreement or disagreement using a prearticle + NP. Use <u>some</u>, <u>most</u>, <u>none</u> (<u>any</u>), <u>all</u>, <u>much</u>, <u>many</u>, <u>a little</u> or <u>a few</u>. Use each at least one time.

Ex: People like entertainment.

Yes. All of the people like entertainment.

People love work.

No. Most of the people do not love work.

1. Parents should arrange their children's marriages.

2. American dating customs are changing.

3. Kate spends her money on her boyfriend.

4. Wedding ceremonies are beautiful.

5. They worked all night.

6. Music for weddings is usually slow and soft.

7. Marriages in my country are always happy.

8. You danced every night last week.

9. People in single's bars like loud music.

10. His friends went to the movies last night.

11. Young people in the U.S. do not have fun.

12. Harry did his homework during the party.

13. A friend's advice is never good.

14. We ate too much last night.

15. Single's bars have "gimmicks."

GRAMMAR 2:   Ought to, Might Have to

Discovery: 1. You ought to try a single's bar. He ought to also.
              2. They might meet people at school. She might also.
              3. I have to leave early. John has to also.

A. Look at sentences 1. In the two sentences, did the verb change? _____

B. Look at sentences 2. Did the verb change here? _____

C. Look at sentences 3. Did the verb change here? _____

What is the form when the subject is I, you, we, or they? _____

What is the form when the subject is he, she, or it? _____

GENERALIZATION

Form:

ought to ⎫
might   ⎬ + simple verb
have/has to ⎭

I ought to go out tonight.
He might go with me.
He has to go.
I have to wait for him.

Ought to and might never change form

Have to changes with the subject. It can
also be in the past tense and future.

The bars have to close.
John has to go.
He had to leave early last night.
He will have to borrow a car.

GENERALIZATION CONTINUED ON NEXT PAGE

Negative = $\begin{cases}\text{might not} \\ \underline{\text{do not have to}}\end{cases}$	We might not go out tonight.
	John does not have to leave early. We do not have to stay. We did not have to talk to her.
People do not usually use ought in negative sentences. Use <u>should</u>.	I ought to go. I should not go.
Use:	
<u>ought to</u> = it is a good idea. (like <u>should</u>)	It is a good idea to go. I ought to go.
<u>might</u> = possibility	Maybe I will go tomorrow. I might go tomorrow.
<u>have to</u> = necessity	I need a good grade. I will have to study.

PRACTICE

Exercise 4:   Rewrite the following sentences using the verb in parentheses.

Ex: Parents arrange their children's marriages. (ought to)

Parents ought to arrange their children's marriages.

1.   Mike spends a little money on his girlfriend. (ought to)

2.   We like their music. (might)

3.   Many of the single's bars have "gimmicks." (have to)

4.   You meet new people every night. (ought to)

5.   He meets some people downtown every night. (have to)

6.   Jane is going to meet her friends at the laundromat. (might)

7.   We spend much of our time at parties. (ought to)

8.   My friend's parents arranged her marriage. (have to)

9.   Joe likes my friends. (might)

10.   A wedding ceremony is long. (have to)

11.   People meet other people in a variety of ways. (ought to)

12.   Joanne's wedding will be elaborate. (have to)

13.   Music for weddings is classical or modern. (might)

14.   Gary took his girlfriend to the movies. (have to)

15.   A young person dates when he is thirteen or fourteen. (might)

Exercise 5: Rewrite your answers to Exercise 4. Change them to the negative form.

Ex: Parents ought to arrange their children's marriages.

Parents should not arrange their children's marriages.

Exercise 6: Fill in the blank with the correct form of the correct verb. Use the hint in parentheses to decide.

Ex: Joan is getting married in August.

She _*has to*_____ make the arrangements. (necessity)

1. Paul met a nice woman last night.

   He _____ get her phone number. (good idea)

2. Cindy is thinking about food for her wedding reception.

   She _____ choose hot or cold food. (possibility)

3. Some people were impolite to René and Marta.

   They _____ ignore those people. (good idea)

4. Bob is late for an appointment with his friends.

   He _____ hurry. (necessity)

5. The bartender charged Charles too much money.

   Charles _____ hit the bartender. (bad idea)

6. Bill was impolite to some people a few minutes ago.

   He _____ apologize to them. (necessity)

7. Kathy has two tickets for the football game.

   She _____ take Ali. (possibility)

8. Sara's wedding is beginning in a few minutes.

   She _____ decide very quickly. (necessity)

9. Gary's new girlfriend invited him to dinner.

   He _____ bring a gift. (no necessity)

10. Cindy wants to give her fiancé a birthday gift.

    She _____ give him a shirt or tie. (possibility)

11. My friends are late for lunch.

    I _____ wait for them. (possible not to)

12. George wants to marry Jenny.

    He _____ talk to her parents. (good idea)

****

MORE PRACTICE

Exercise 7: Answer the following questions using a prearticle + NP.

Ex: Do people like parties in your country?

Most of the people in my country like parties.

1. Do you go out with the people in your writing class?
2. Do you see a lot of American movies?
3. Do you see a lot of French movies?
4. Do the people in your country marry at a young age?
5. Are the husbands the head of the family in your country?
6. Do married women with children work in your country?
7. Did you spend your time with friends last night?
8. Is the music on your radio nice?
9. Did you spend your money in one place yesterday?
10. Were these questions difficult?

Exercise 8: READ AND COMMENT. Read each sentence. Write 3 more sentences as additional information. Use prearticles and have to/ought to/might when possible.

Ex: I met some new people last night.

A. *I might invite them to a party.*
B. *Most of them were very nice!*
C. *Much of the time we danced and sang.*

1. Weddings are beautiful in my country.

   A.

   B.

   C.

2. Young people have different activities in my country.

   A.

   B.

   C.

3. John is always rude to people.

    A.

    B.

    C.

4. Dating customs are (not) changing in my country.

    A.

    B.

    C.

5. Marriage is (not) important.

    A.

    B.

    C.

Exercise 9: Write 3 paragraphs about marriages in your country. Use the outline below as a guide. Add other information if necessary.

1. How do two people become engaged? (ask the parents? ring? date a long or short time? parents arrange it?)

2. Describe the marriage ceremony. (religious? governmental? customs and traditions?)

3. Describe the typical marriage briefly. (husband and wife roles? children soon or not? divorce possible?)

    Begin: *In my country, people usually ...*

COMPOSITION

Describe the ways men meet women (or women meet men) in your country. What do you think are the best ways?

LESSON 17   Comparison (<u>Like</u>, <u>The same as</u>, <u>Different from</u>)
            Introductory <u>There</u>

INTRODUCTION

American Food

There are many types of food in the United States. A lot of food is like food
in other countries. For example, Americans love Italian spaghetti, German **sauer-**
kraut, and Slavic pierogies. This is because many Americans are from these other
countries.

But there is also American food. The typical American meal almost always
includes meat and potatoes. Until prices became so high, the meat was usually
beef -- roasts or steaks. Now it is chicken, hamburger, and pork.

Hamburgers and french fries are popular at lunch time. Hamburgers are like
meatballs, but they are flat. Americans eat them with lettuce, tomato, pickles,
and a sauce. It is the same as a salad and meat on a bun. Hamburgers are very
different from other food. For this reason, many foreign visitors hate them.
Americans like them because they are easy to make, quick to eat, and cheap.

GRAMMAR 1: Comparison (<u>Like</u>, <u>The same as</u>, <u>Different from</u>)

    Discovery: 1. American food is like food in other countries.
                  2. A hamburger is the same as a salad and meat on a bun.
                  3. Hamburgers are very different from other food.

A. Look at the sentences above. Which two things are similar?

    _____ and _____

    Which two things are the same? _____ and _____

    Which two things are different? _____ and _____

B. Do we write the comparison words <u>like</u>, <u>the same as</u>, or <u>different from</u>
    before the first member or the second member of the comparison?

    _____

135

GENERALIZATION

Form:

The comparison words like, the same as, and different from come before the second member of the comparison.

                    1   2
A hamburger is like a meatball.
                    1   2
A salad is the same as greens.
                              1
American food looks different
                    2
from Chinese food.

Use:

like = similar but not exactly the same.

Cabbage is like lettuce.

We also use it for figurative phrases.

This food tastes like wood.

the same as = equal, same

A drink is the same as a beverage.

different from = unequal, different

A meal is different from a snack.

PRACTICE

Exercise 1:   Fill in the blank with like, the same as, or different from, according to the cue in parentheses.

Ex: This restaurant's food is ___*like*___ a jail's food. (similar)

1.   The meat tastes _____ paper. (figurative)

2.   Liquor is _____ spirits. (equal)

3.   Butter is _____ margarine. (unequal)

4.   Candy is _____ sweets. (equal)

5.   Some American food tastes _____ Italian food. (similar)

6.   Mashed potatoes are _____ whipped potatoes. (equal)

7.   American food is _____ Arabic food. (unequal)

8.   My wife eats _____ a horse. (figurative)

9.   An appetizer _____ a dessert. (unequal)

10.   An entre is _____ a main course. (equal)

11.   Beef is _____ veal. (unequal)

12.   Hot dogs are _____ sausages. (similar)

Exercise 2: Write sentences from the following phrases using <u>like</u>, <u>the same as</u>, or <u>different from</u> according to the cue in parentheses.

Ex: wife/eat/horse (figurative)

My wife eats like a horse.

1. rabbit/taste/chicken (similar)

2. snack/be/meal (unequal)

3. hamburger/be/steak (unequal)

4. dinner/be/supper (equal *)

5. turkey/be/chicken (similar)

6. daughter/eat/bird (figurative)

7. side dish/be/salad (unequal)

8. pasta/be/noodles (equal)

9. brunch/be/breakfast and lunch (similar)

10. American food/be/Latin American food (unequal)

GRAMMAR 2: Introductory <u>There</u>

Discovery: 1. There are many kinds of American food.
2. There is meat at almost every meal.

A. Look at sentence 1 above. Which word in the sentence does the verb agree with? _____

B. Look at sentence 2. Which word in the sentence does the verb agree with? _____

GENERALIZATION

Form: <u>There</u> + <u>be</u> + subject + completer   There are many kinds of food.
                                                        There is meat for most meals.

The verb agrees with the subject.   There will be a dinner tomorrow.
It can be in any tense.

Use: <u>There</u> starts sentences when the subject
occurs later. It is a stylistic device and,   An Arabic dish was on the
therefore, it is the writer's choice to use   menu.
it. However, the subject must be indefinite.   There was an Arabic dish on
                                                  the menu.
This form often occurs at the beginning   (See the INTRODUCTION at the
of writing.   beginning of this lesson.)

---

* in some dialects

PRACTICE

Exercise 3: Fill in the blank with the correct form of <u>be</u>. Pay attention to the time expressions.

Ex: There _*Was*_ live music at the restaurant last night.

1. There _____ meatballs in spaghetti sauce.
2. Sometimes, there _____ cheese on a hamburger.
3. There _____ many kinds of food in the U.S. today.
4. At the next international party, there _____ "tabuli" and "lubia."
5. There _____ pizzas at the party last night.
6. There _____ a delicious food in Venezuela called "arepas."
7. There _____ a lot of fast food restaurants in the U.S.
8. In Mexico, there _____ tacos and burritos.
9. There _____ a lot of wine at the next party.
10. There _____ many spicy dishes in the Arabic countries.

Exercise 4: Write sentences from the following phrases using <u>introductory "there."</u>

Ex: live music/restaurant/last week

There was live music at the restaurant last week.

1. fast food restaurants/big cities
2. very little spice/American food
3. potatoes/every meal
4. a nice restaurant/my home
5. potato chips and beer/party/tomorrow night
6. several popular vegetables/U.S.
7. horrible food/that restaurant/last week
8. vegetarians/my country
9. a fly/my soup
10. several choices/for an appetizer

****

MORE PRACTICE

Exercise 5: Read each item, then <u>truthfully</u> compare it to something using <u>like</u>, <u>the same as</u> or <u>different from</u>.

Ex: rabbit

Eating a rabbit is like eating a pet!

1. hamburgers
2. my recipes
3. chicken
4. American food
5. salad
6. restaurants
7. my taste for food
8. food in my country

Exercise 6: READ AND COMMENT. Read each statement. Write 2 more statements as additional information. Use comparisons and <u>there</u> whenever possible.

Ex: Food in my country is delicious.

A. *It is different from food in the U.S.*
B. *There are more spices in our food.*

1. Hamburgers are horrible/wonderful.

A.

B.

2. I like some American restaurants.

A.

B.

3. My favorite food is _____.

A.

B.

4. American food surprised me when I came here.

A.

B.

5. We always have food at our parties.

A.

B.

Exercise 7: Write a short composition about food in the U.S. Use the following outline as a guide.

1. What did you think of the food when you first came here? Describe some of your experiences when you ate some foods for the first time.

2. What is the <u>worst</u> American food? Why? What is the <u>best</u> American food? Why?

3. Do you know how to cook? Did you know how when you arrived? Do you often eat American food now or do you cook food from your country? If you cook your country's food, how do you find the necessary ingredients?

Begin: *I thought American food was...*

COMPOSITION

Describe the foods and eating habits of the people in your country.

LESSON 18   <u>May/Must</u>
            <u>Manner Expressions</u>

INTRODUCTION

How to Shop for Food

These days, food can be very expensive, but there are a lot of ways to save
money at the supermarket. One way is by looking for sales. Every week, a lot of
stores advertise special prices for some of their products in the newspaper or on
television. These sales usually last only a short time (one week) but if the
stores don't have the product during that time, they must give it to you later for
the sale price.

Sometimes you can save money with coupons in the newspaper or magazines. By
using these coupons, you may save several dollars each time you shop.

Another way to save money is by comparing brands. Each store has national
brands and a store brand. Store brands are cheaper but they have the same quality
usually. They are cheaper because their advertising costs are very low. You
can compare the quality of national and store brands by looking at the label on
the package. The label will tell you the ingredients in each package and it will
give you nutritional information. Some stroes also sell generic (no brand) products.
These are usually very cheap but the quality is not the same. However, they are
nutritious.

By shopping carefully and patiently, you can buy food without spending too
much money. Just watch the newspapers and the labels on the packages.

GRAMMAR 1: <u>May/Must</u>

Discovery: 1. They must give it to you later.
            2. He may save several dollars.

A. What are the complete verbs in 1 and 2 above? _____

                                                   _____

B. Does the form of the first verb ever change? _____

C. What do you think is the negative form of these verb phrases? _____

141

GENERALIZATION

Form:

$\left.\begin{array}{l} \underline{may} \\ \underline{must} \end{array}\right\}$ + simple verb

You must mix it quickly.
The water may be cold.

Negative = $\left.\begin{array}{l} \underline{may} \\ \underline{must} \end{array}\right\}$ + $\underline{not}$ + simple verb

It may not be too hot.

Use:

The usual meanings in writing are:

$\underline{may}$ = possibility

Warm water may ruin the pie crust.

$\underline{must}$ = necessity
deduction

You must bake the cake immediately.
The cake fell. The oven must be too hot.

$\underline{must\ not}$ = $\left\{\begin{array}{l} forbidden \\ deduction \end{array}\right.$

You must not use a coupon after the date on it.
Joan won't take the apartment. She must not like it.

NOTE: $\underline{might}$ also means possibility

We$\left\{\begin{array}{l} might \\ may \end{array}\right\}$bake a cake.

$\underline{have\ to}$ also means necessity

They$\left\{\begin{array}{l} have\ to \\ must \end{array}\right\}$shop carefully

PRACTICE

Exercise 1: Rewrite the following sentences using $\underline{may}$ or $\underline{must}$.

Ex: A coupon saves money. (may)

A coupon may save money.

1. You stir the eggs quickly. (must)

_____

2. We buy national or store brands. (may)

_____

3. I use very little shortening. (must)

_____

4. He changes stores every month. (may)

_____

5. Jane reads the advertisements for new apartments. (must)

_____

6. Joe cooks for his roommates. (must)

_____

7. Mary watches a lot of television during her vacation. (may)

_____

8. My friend finds a new sale every day. (may)

_____

9. We read the labels on the packages. (must)

_____

10. Kathy buys vitamins for her health. (may)

_____

Exercise 2: Rewrite the sentences in Exercise 1. Change them to the negative form.

Ex: A coupon may save money.

A coupon may not save money.

Exercise 3: Fill in the blank with the affirmative or negative form of <u>may</u> or <u>must</u>. Use the cue to decide.

Ex: You *must* add the water after the flour. (necessity)

1. A recipe _____ call for water or milk. (possibility)

2. A supermarket _____ give a raincheck during a sale. (necessity)

3. Bread dough _____ rise for several hours. (necessity)

4. Your oven _____ heat to the correct temperature. (possible not)

5. Product labels _____ also give nutritional information (necessity)

6. Generic foods _____ have the same quality as other brands. (possibility)

7. Stores _____ have "fake" sales. (forbidden)

8. Some labels _____ list the product's ingredients. (possible not)

9. My wife says, "Pie-crust _____ be thin and flaky." (necessity)

10. Meat _____ stay out of the refrigerator too long. (forbidden)

Exercise 4: Fill in the blank with a model verb (<u>can</u>, <u>will</u>, <u>should</u>, <u>ought</u> <u>to</u>, <u>have to</u>, <u>might</u>, <u>may</u>, <u>must</u>) according to the information under the blank. More than one answer will be possible sometimes.

How to Bake a Carrot Cake*

All of the ingredients _____*should*_____ be about 70°F. Measure 1 cup of
                          (good idea)

flour into a bowl. The bowl _____ be very large. Add 1
                              (not necessity)

teaspoon of baking soda, 1 teaspoon of baking powder, 1 teaspoon of cinnamon,

and 1/2 teaspoon of salt. Mix these very well. In a separate bowl, mix 2/3

cup vegetable oil, 1 cup of sugar and 2 eggs. Add this mixture to the dry

ingredients but you _____ stir it slowly. You _____
                      (necessity)   (bad idea)

allow bubbles to form because they _____ cause holes in the cake.
                                      (possibility)

Now grate several carrots. The gratings _____ be very small.
                                            (good idea)

You _____ need 1 1/2 cups of carrots. Stir the carrots into the batter
      (future)

slowly. Last, add chopped nuts. You _____ want to use pecans or
                                         (possible)

you _____ prefer walnuts. You _____ also forget the
      (possible)   (able)

nuts if you don't like them. Put the batter into an eight-inch square pan and

bake the cake at 325°F for about 30 minutes. When it is cool, cover it with

cream cheese frosting. It _____ be delicious!
                             (promise)

*Recipe from Irma S. Rombauer and Marion Rombauer Becker, <u>The Joy of Cooking</u>
 (Indianapolis: The Bobbs-Merrill Co., Inc., 1975), p. 684.

GRAMMAR 2: Manner Expressions

Discovery: How do you shop for food?

      1. Slowly and patiently.
      2. By looking for the bargains.
      3. With coupons from the newspaper.
          Without my husband.
      4. Without thinking!

A. Look at number 1 above. What kinds of words are <u>slowly</u> and <u>carefully</u>?
_____ How were they formed? _____ + _____

B. Look at 2, the phrase "by looking." How was it formed?
_____ + _____ + _____

C. Look at 3, the phrase "with coupons." How was it formed? _____
+ _____

Look at the phrase "without my husband." How was it formed?
_____ + _____

D. Look at 4, the phrase "without thinking." How was it formed? _____ +
_____

GENERALIZATION

Form:

1. Many adverbs = adjective +<u>-ly</u>   How does he work?
                                   He works quickly.

    Adjectives that end with <u>y</u>, change
    <u>y</u> to <u>i</u> and add <u>-ly</u>.   easy   easily
                                busy   busily

    Note the irregular forms:
        good   well
        hard   hard   Mary works hard and well.
     straight straight
        fast   fast

2. <u>by</u> + verb + <u>-ing</u>   He works by planning a schedule.

3. <u>with</u>(<u>out</u>) + noun phrase   He works with a secretary.
                                     He works without a desk.

4. <u>without</u> + verb + <u>-ing</u>   He works without stopping.

Use: These expressions explain how something is
      done. They describe the action.

PRACTICE

Exercise 5: Complete the following sentences with an <u>adverb</u>. Use the adjective in parentheses.

Ex: Jane cooks very __*Well*__. (good)

1. Bill looked very _____ for an apartment. (hard)

2. People can save money _____. (easy)

3. I read my lease _____ before I signed it. (complete)

4. Beat the egg yolks _____ with a fork. (quick)

5. Mix the flour in _____. (thorough)

6. I always pay my rent _____. (prompt)

7. Good shoppers _____ compare products before they purchase them. (careful)

8. Joe shops _____ and _____. (patient, shrewd)

Exercise 6: Fill in the blank with an <u>adverb</u> to describe actions or an <u>adjective</u> to describe nouns. Only one is possible. Be sure the story makes sense.

Barbara Horton needs a __*new*__ apartment. Her _____ apartment

is too _____ and _____. She will read the newspapers _____

and look for _____ possibilities. By _____ reading the

advertisements, she might find a/an _____ apartment. After

she finds one in the paper, she will phone the landlord and go see it. She will

look at it _____. She will _____ consider the

cost, the location, and its condition. If she takes it, she will make a _____

list of its problems and she will ask her _____ landlord to sign the

list. Later, if she moves, she can _____ receive her security deposit

from the landlord when he compares the list to the apartment's _____

condition. Then she and her landlord can end their relationship _____.

Exercise 7: Complete the following sentences with <u>by + verb + -ing</u>. Use the verb in parentheses.

Ex: She cooks _*by opening*_ boxes. (open)

1. I shop _____ for bargains. (watch)

2. Bob chooses products _____ at the labels. (look)

3. _____ patiently and carefully, we can save money. (shop)

4. I always prepare food _____ a recipe. (follow)

5. John prepares food _____ the ingredients. (guess)

6. My family saves money _____ coupons. (use)

7. _____ the date on packages, you can choose fresh food. (check)

8. _____ the ingredients on the label, you can compare brands. (read)

Exercise 8: Complete the following sentences with <u>with(out) + Noun Phrase</u>. Use the noun in parentheses. Be careful with the meaning!

Ex: Joe got into his apartment _*with his key*_. (key)

1. You cannot find a good apartment _____. (reliable information)

2. Jane shops _____. (calculator)

3. I found an apartment _____. (friend's help)

4. I pay my rent _____. (check)

5. Many people fry potatoes _____. (butter and salt)

6. Jane went to see an apartment _____. (list of questions)

7. She remembered the recipe so well that she cooked the food _____. (it)

8. Bob signed the lease _____ and he was sorry later. (family's advice)

Exercise 9: Complete the following sentences with <u>without + verb + -ing</u> and a completer if necessary. Use the verb in parentheses.

Ex: Jane signed the lease _*without asking*_ for advice. (ask)

1. Mike makes pizzas _____. (follow)

2. Joan paid her security deposit _____. (write)

3. _____, it is hard to save money. (use)

4. People should not take apartments _____. (see)

5. You may not find a good apartment _____. (look)

6. I always prepare food _____. (use)

7. Joe bought the more expensive product _____. (read)

8. _____, it is not easy to find apartments. (look)

Exercise 10: Complete the following sentences with a manner expression. Be careful with the meaning!

Ex: I eat *(with my fingers)(quickly)* , etc.

1. Joe shops _____.

2. I find the bargains _____.

3. He always cooks _____.

4. We found an apartment _____.

5. I save money at the supermarket _____.

6. I prepare my favorite food _____.

7. _____, we can be sure to have fresh products.

8. Mary can protect her security deposit _____.

****

MORE PRACTICE

Exercise 11: Answer the following questions with a complete sentence.

1. How do you shop for food?

2. Must food companies list ingredients on packages in your country?

3. How can you find the best food bargains?

4. What should you do if a store has no more sale products, but the sale isn't finished?

5. How can you save money when you shop for food?

Exercise 12: <u>READ AND COMMENT</u>. Read each sentence. Write 2 more sentences as additional information. Use examples of modals and manner expressions.

Ex: Nancy only buys things that are on sale.

A. *She may save a lot of money.*

B. *She finds the sales by looking in the newspapers.*

1. John is a gourmet cook.

   A.

   B.

2. Jane needs to save more money on food.

   A.

   B.

3. Bob is looking for a new apartment.

   A.

   B.

4. Jim's landlord will not return his security deposit.

   A.

   B.

5. People should shop for food very carefully.

   A.

   B.

Exercise 13: Write a short composition "How to Find an Apartment." Some ways to get information are:

   A. Newspapers (city and school)
   B. Friends or relatives
   C. Off-campus housing office (has information about area apartments)
   D. Notices on bulletin boards

Include your ideas. How did you get an apartment? Use examples of modals and manner expressions.

Begin: *In order to find an apartment, you should first...*

COMPOSITION

Choose your favorite food and explain how to make it. (Be careful! Your teacher may want to try it!)

LESSON 19   Modal Questions
            Yes/No, Wh-

INTRODUCTION

Request for Information

Universities often have students who are available to answer new or prospective students' questions. Sylvia Hernandez is planning to study for her Master's Degree at a large northeastern university. She is writing to one of the student "mentors" for information about the campus and the city.

July 6, 1981

Dear Patty,

   Ms. Miller of the Student Affairs Office gave me your name and address because I need some information about the university and the city. I will begin to study there this fall and I have so many questions.

   First, I should tell you that I am from Venezuela. Can you tell me about the foreign student organizations on campus? Are there any? If so, will you please send me their addresses?

   My biggest concern is living arrangements. Must I live in the dormitory? If not, how might I find a nice but inexpensive apartment? I can pay $175. I'm sure this is not enough to live alone. What should I do to find a roommate? Do I have to have any extra money if I get an apartment? If I must live in the dormitory, how can I cut the cost? Will the cost of the meals be included in the price of the room? If not, what can I do to save money on food?

   I realize there are a lot of questions for you to answer here. I really appreciate the time you are taking. Thank you.

                              Sincerely,

                              Silvia Hernández
                              Silvia Hernández

GRAMMAR 1: Yes/No Questions

Discovery: Can you tell me about the foreign student organizations?

151

A. Notice the positions of the modal verb (<u>can</u>), the main verb, and the subject. How is this type of question formed? _____ + _____ + _____.

Do I have to have any extra money?

B. Notice the verb phrase. How is the question formed with this modal? _____ + _____ + _____ + _____.

GENERALIZATION

Form:

$\left.\begin{array}{l}\underline{can} \\ \underline{will} \\ \underline{should} \\ \underline{may} \\ \underline{might} \\ \underline{must}\end{array}\right\}$ + subject + main verb   Must I live in the dormitory?

<u>do</u> + subject + <u>have to</u> + main verb   Do I have to live in the dormi-
                                                          tory?

Use: Use this question form when   Will the cost of the meals be
      you expect a <u>yes</u> or <u>no</u> answer.   included?   Yes (No)
      People usually do not use <u>ought</u>
      <u>to</u> in questions. Use <u>should</u>.

PRACTICE

Exercise 1: Write questions from the following phrases. Use a modal with the meaning in parentheses. Try to use examples of all the modals you have learned.

Ex: I/stay/apartment   (necessity)

Do I have to stay in an apartment?

1. I/take/loan/from the bank   (good idea)

2. I/ask/you/question   (permission)

3. they/cancel/class   (possibility)

4. the administration/give/receipt   (necessity)

5. student/have/visitors/room   (ability)

6. student/live/dormitory/or apartment   (good idea)

7. I/live/dormitory   (necessity)

8. you/answer/questions   (determination)

9. I/find/inexpensive apartment   (possibility)

10. student/pay for/meals   (necessity)

11. you/help/me   (ability)

12. lease/be/a year long   (necessity)

13. they/include/cost of the meals   (ability)

14. there/be/a list of roommates   (possibility)

15. students/take/literature classes   (necessity)

GRAMMAR 2: Wh- Questions, Completer

Discovery: 1. He should do something to find an apartment.
             2. What should he do?

A. Notice the question form above. Does what refer to the subject or completer?

_____. How is this type of question formed? _____ +

_____ + _____ + _____.

```
┌─────────────────────────────────────────────────────────────────────────┐
│  GENERALIZATION                                                           │
│                                                                           │
│  Form:                                                                    │
│                                                                           │
│              ⎛ can   ⎞                                                     │
│              ⎜ will  ⎟                                                     │
│  wh- word + ⎨ should ⎬ + subject + main verb    How can I cut the cost?   │
│              ⎜ may    ⎟                                                     │
│              ⎜ might  ⎟                                                     │
│              ⎝ must   ⎠                                                     │
│                                                                           │
│  wh- word + do + subject + have to + main verb   What do I have to do?     │
│                                                                           │
│  Use:  Use this question form when you    How can I cut the cost?          │
│        expect a piece of information in   (by using coupons.)              │
│        the answer.  The wh- word refers                                   │
│        to the completer in the question                                   │
└─────────────────────────────────────────────────────────────────────────┘
```

PRACTICE

Exercise 2: Make questions about the completer using the following statements.

Ex: He can do something to save money.

What can he do to save money?

1. Joe will go somewhere to study.

2. Mary might find an apartment sometime.

3. He should do something to save money.

4. Bob has to do something soon.

5. His family will visit him sometime.

6. Katerina might go somewhere first.

7. They have to talk to somebody about living arrangements.

8. Luis must send an application somewhere.

9. Bill must find something before he leaves.

10. The students have to ask somebody about their schedules.

11. They may go somewhere after class.

12. Sylvia should write to somebody for answers.

13. They can send a letter sometime.

14. Cindy has to write somewhere for advice.

15. The mentor will send Gustavo something.

GRAMMAR 3: Wh- Questions, Subject

    Discovery: 1. Somebody can help her.
                 2. Who can help her?

    A. Notice the question form above. Does who refer to the subject or completer? _____ . How is this type of question formed? _____ + _____ + _____ .

```
┌─────────────────────────────────────────────────────────────────┐
│ GENERALIZATION                                                    │
│                                                                   │
│ Form:              ⎧ can   ⎫                                      │
│                    │ will  │                                      │
│      wh- word +    │ should│  + main verb  Who can help the student?│
│                    │ may   │                                      │
│                    │ might │                                      │
│                    ⎩ must  ⎭                                      │
│                                                                   │
│ wh- word + has to + main verb        Who has to save money?       │
│                                                                   │
│ Use:  This question form also asks for    What can save money?    │
│       a piece of information.  The wh-      (Using coupons.)       │
│       word refers to the subject in the   Who has to cut costs?   │
│       question.                             (Silvia has to.)       │
└─────────────────────────────────────────────────────────────────┘
```

PRACTICE

Exercise 3:   Make questions about the subject using the following statements.

Ex: Somebody will write to a mentor.

Who will write to a mentor?

1. Somebody can cut costs well.

2. Something has to arrive at the bank first.

3. Somebody might invite Sylvia to the meetings.

4. Something will cost extra money.

5. Somebody must answer the questions.

6. Something may come in the mail.

7. Somebody should save money by cooking in the room.

8. Something has to be cheap but comfortable.

9. Something might cost too much.

10. Somebody will help the students with their questions.

Exercise 4:   Make questions about the subject or completer using the following statements.

Ex: Sylvia will write to somebody.

Who will Sylvia write to?

1. The application must arrive somewhere first.

2. The advisor will help somebody with his problems.

3. He might invite somebody to the meetings.

4. Somebody will visit him tonight.

5. Something should arrive tomorrow.

6. Somebody has to ask the advisor about his schedule.

7. Bill must talk to his advisor sometime.

8. Something might cost too much.

9. They may go to the library sometime.

10. Tuition might cost too much somewhere.

11. Somebody will go to Wisconsin to study.

12. Cindy has to write to the university for something.

Exercise 5: Make questions about the subject or completer using the following statements. Be careful with the use of <u>do</u>.

Ex: Ralqui works somewhere.

Where does Ralqui work?

Jane is talking to somebody.

Who is Jane talking to?

1. Sylvia is going to go somewhere.

2. Somebody talked to the banker.

3. Cindy wrote somewhere for advice.

4. They will mail the applications sometime.

5. Juana is going somewhere tomorrow.

6. Somebody saved money by cooking in the room.

7. Michele can write to somebody for information.

8. Bill goes somewhere every day before class.

9. Somebody is writing a letter to a mentor.

10. Roberto went to Yale University sometime.

11. Somebody answered all of Jawaher's questions.

12. Janet is going to study somewhere next month.

13. Mary might find something soon.

14. Jane goes to school somewhere.

15. Somebody will send Abdalla information.

****

MORE PRACTICE

Exercise 6: READ AND COMMENT. Read each statement. Write three questions to obtain necessary information. Use modal verbs whenever possible.

Ex: Jose needs information about tuition payments.

A. *Can he pay a little each month?*

B. *Where should he pay the bill?*

C. *Who does he have to talk to about extensions?*

1. Sylvia wants to know about living arrangements.

    A.

    B.

    C.

2. I am interested in foreign student organizations.

    A.

    B.

    C.

3. Marco needs to save money.

    A.

    B.

    C.

4. Felipe and Ramón want information about the campus health center.

    A.

    B.

    C.

5. Abdulaziz wants to know how to make friends.

    A.

    B.

    C.

6. Narumon needs information about finding roommates.

    A.

    B.

    C.

7. Mohammad needs help with his schedule of classes.

   A.

   B.

   C.

8. Irena cannot decide on a major.

   A.

   B.

   C.

Exercise 7:   Imagine that you lived in one American city for two years. During that time, you became very good friends with an American. Now you are getting ready to start classes at a university in another city. Write to your friend. Tell him/her how you are doing and ask him/her about possibilities, necessities, rules, and for advice. Some things you might wonder about are below. You may add other ideas.

course work (choosing courses or a major)
schedule
apartments
costs of clothing, food, housing
how to make friends

Begin:

(Today's date)

Dear...

COMPOSITION

Write a letter requesting information from a university which you plan to attend or a company where you hope to work. Request the information you think you will need.

LESSON 20   Subject It
              Past time + Ago
              Verb + Indirect Object + Direct Object

INTRODUCTION

Health Fads*

Every year, millions of dollars are spent on health in the U.S., excluding
bills for doctors, hospitals, and medication. Many Americans spend hundreds of
dollars on vitamins, diets, exercise machines, organic foods** or jogging***
equipment. One of these fads, taking vatamins, can be very helpful, but it can
also be dangerous as well as costly.

Several years ago, Dr. Linus Pauling suggested that vitamin C might prevent
colds. Now a lot of people take large doses of this vitamin. Many people also
take large doses of other vitamins for everything from energy to wrinkles. But
it can be dangerous to do this. For example, too much vitamin A may cause mental
unbalance. Yet vitamins are easily bought with the blessings of the companies
that produce them. Pharmacies sell people vitamins without prescriptions.

Of course vitamins can have a good effect on health. Mothers give their
children vitamins and people credit vitamins with the size and health of children
these days. There are also multiple vitamin tablets which people take to supplement vitamins from food. Although most Americans have plenty to eat, it is difficult
for them to get all of the necessary vitamins because they often eat foods low in
nutrition.

Two generations ago, people received most of their vitamins from food. Now
a major part of them may come from a bottle of vitamin tablets.

---

  * Fad is a new style or fashion.
 ** Organic foods are grown without chemicals.
*** Jogging is running for exercise.

159

GRAMMAR 1: Subject _It_

   Discovery: It can be dangerous to take large doses of vitamins.

   A. Look at the sentence above. What does _it_ mean? What can be dangerous?

   _____

GENERALIZATION

Form:

_It_ + _be_ + adjective + _to_ + Verb Phrase   It is easy to be healthy.

Use:

This is another way to postpone the   {To take} pills can be unsafe.
real subject of the sentence. It is   {Taking }
a stylistic variation.
                                           It can be unsafe to take pills.

Compare subject _it_ with introductory _there_.

_It_ postpones verb constructions.   It is difficult to get the
                                              necessary vitamins.

There postpones noun phrases.   There are dangerous fads
                                              about health.

PRACTICE

   Exercise 1: Rewrite the following sentences using subject _it_.

        Ex: To be healthy is easy.

        It is easy to be healthy.

1. To exercise daily is difficult.

2. To jog early in the morning is wonderful.

3. Walking alone in a woods is peaceful.

4. Eating the proper foods is healthful.

5. Taking too much medication can be very dangerous.

6. To lose weight by taking diet pills can be unsafe.

7. Swimming is exciting.

8. Exercising too much can be unhealthful.

9. Having a big dinner with family and friends is enjoyable.

10. Eating only vegetables might be very healthful.

11. Exercising with friends is fun.

12. Jogging without the proper shoes might be very painful.

13. To follow fad diets is dangerous and expensive.

14. Taking diet pills can be very unsafe.

15. Dieting without a doctor's advice is stupid.

Exercise 2: Complete the following sentences with a to + verb phrase construction. Use the verb in parentheses.

Ex: It is easy *to jog four miles*____. (jog)

1. It is fun _____. (eat)

2. It is dangerous _____. (exercise)

3. It is hard _____. (jog)

4. It is expensive _____. (buy)

5. It is smart _____. (eat)

6. It is good _____. (supplement)

7. It is easy _____. (run)

8. It is helpful _____. (talk)

9. It is interesting _____. (read)

10. It is difficult _____. (diet)

GRAMMAR 2: Past Time + Ago

Discovery: John went on a diet three weeks ago.

A. Look at the sentence above. What tense is the first part? _____

What is the time expression? _____

How is it formed? _____ + _____

GENERALIZATION

Form: quantity + time word + <u>ago</u>

one week ago
an hour ago
several days ago
six years ago
a few hours ago

Use: Use this type of time
expression to show a
point of time in the past.

It is Tuesday. We went to
a health spa on Sunday.
We went two days ago.

PRACTICE

Exercise 3: Rewrite the following sentences using a past time + <u>ago</u>
expression.

Ex: Jane went to the spa at 1:00.

She went two hours ago.

1. You started a diet last week.

2. Bill bought a tennis racket on Saturday.

3. Joe became a vegetarian last year.

4. Kathy saw her doctor at 12:00.

5. José began taking vitamins last month.

6. I ran two miles this morning.

7. Mike lost forty pounds the year before last.

8. Gary took his last diet pill at 8:00 this morning.

9. Tom started growing his tomatoes last Wednesday.

10. Alice followed the fads when she was a teenager.

11. Jim jogged to the store at 1:00.

12. Bill began eating organic foods in 1976.

GRAMMAR 3: Verb + Indirect Object + Direct Object

Discovery: She bought her child some vitamins.

A. Look at the sentence above. What did she buy? _____
Who will receive them? _____

B. Is the receiver first or second after the verb? _____

GENERALIZATION

Form: Verb + IO + DO   Mothers give their children vitamins.

Use: The indirect object is the   Jane gave her friend running shoes.
      recipient of the direct object.   I.O.   D.O.
      The direct object is directly   Bill told the doctor the problem.
      affected by the action of   I.O.   D.O.
      the verb.
When both types of object are in   Bill told him the problem.
one sentence, the indirect object
can be in pronoun form.

PRACTICE

Exercise 4: Rewrite the following sentences to include the indirect object
             in parentheses.

         Ex: Mothers give vitamins. (their children)

         Mothers give their children vitamins.

1. Jill found a spa. (her husband)

2. Bob left the money. (the doctor)

3. The diet doctor can give a prescription. (the patient)

4. The salesman showed some exercise machines. (the customer)

5. Mike will order salads for dinner. (his wife and children)

6. I am buying some vitamins. (my son)

7. Joe took some organic food. (his girlfriend)

8. Mike is going to teach tennis. (his children)

9. We paid the money for the examination. (the doctor)

10. They showed the new exercises last night. (the students)

11. Kathy got some vegetarian food. (her daughter)

12. They threw the ball across the field. (their teammates)

Exercise 5: Rewrite your answers in exercise 4. Change the indirect objects
             to the completer pronoun. If you cannot know whether to use
             him or her, use him.

         Ex: Mothers give their children vitamins.

         Mothers give them vitamins.

****

MORE PRACTICE

Exercise 6: Answer the following questions using subject <u>it</u>.

1. What is easy in your classes?

It is easy to get good grades in my classes.

2. What is difficult in your classes?

3. What do you usually think is interesting?

4. What is usually fun?

5. What is usually boring?

6. What do you think is dangerous?

7. What do you think is helpful?

8. What is usually funny?

Exercise 7: Answer the following questions using a second object and a time expression with <u>ago</u>.

1. Who did you last write a letter to?

I wrote my family a letter six days ago.

2. When did you last give advice?

3. What did you last show your friend?

4. When did you last give a gift?

5. When did you last leave money?

6. Who did you last order a meal for?

7. Who did you last do a favor for?

8. What did you last buy somebody?

Exercise 8: READ AND COMMENT. Read each sentence then write three more sentences as additional information. Use subject <u>it</u>, past time + <u>ago</u>, or verb + IO + DO whenever possible.

Ex: Jane went on a diet.

    A. *She began a week ago.*
    B. *Her doctor is giving her advice.*
    C. *It will be good for her health.*

1. Joe got some new exercise equipment.

    A.

    B.

    C.

2. Bill had his physical examination.

    A.

    B.

    C.

3. Mike is learning how to play tennis.

    A.

    B.

    C.

4. Sarah takes large doses of vitamins.

    A.

    B.

    C.

5. Martha never eats meat.

    A.

    B.

    C.

6. Mary grows her own vegetables.

   A.

   B.

   C.

7. Kathy is following a fad diet.

   A.

   B.

   C.

8. Bob and Sue exercise together.

   A.

   B.

   C.

Exercise 9: Write a short composition about health habits in your country. Use the following outline as a guide. Use subject <u>it</u>, verb + indirect object + direct object and past time + <u>ago</u> when possible.

1. Describe the health habits of the average person in your country.
2. What special things do people do to be healthy?
3. Are health concerns different now from your parents' or grandparents' time? How?
4. How do you think a person can become and remain healthy?

COMPOSITION

Imagine your family is coming for a visit. What American foods would you choose for them and why?